THE ART
of SILENCE

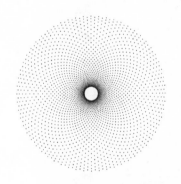

THE ART
of SILENCE

AMBER HATCH

piatkus

PIATKUS

First published in Great Britain in 2017 by Piatkus

Copyright © Amber Hatch 2017

1 3 5 7 9 10 8 6 4 2

The moral right of the author has been asserted.

A CIP catalogue record for this book
is available from the British Library.

ISBN 978-0-349-41812-4

Typeset in Garamond 3 by M Rules
Printed and bound in Great Britain by
Clays Ltd, St Ives plc

Papers used by Piatkus are from well-managed forests
and other responsible sources.

Piatkus
An imprint of
Little, Brown Book Group
Carmelite House
50 Victoria Embankment
London EC4Y 0DZ

An Hachette UK Company
www.hachette.co.uk

www.improvementzone.co.uk

For all those who sense that
more is not the answer

Amber Hatch is a writer, teacher and mindfulness expert, and has been practising daily Buddhist meditation for eight years. She helps organise family retreats at the Samatha centre in Wales and has also helped establish a mindfulness support group for parents in Oxford. She has three children.

Amber has written two parenting books, including *Mindfulness for Parents* (Watkins 2017), and two mindful colouring books in collaboration with her illustrator husband, Alex Ogg.

CONTENTS

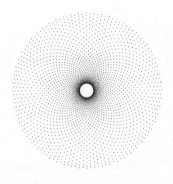

INTRODUCTION

WHAT IS SILENCE?

We all know what silence means. Yet how many of us
have experienced it? The dictionary tells us that silence
is a 'complete absence of sound', but how can we have an
absence of sound? Sound is all around us. It's caused by
vibrations travelling through the air (or other medium),
which in turn make our eardrums vibrate. Our brain

then interprets these vibrations as sounds. We don't live in a vacuum (luckily, as we would perish pretty quickly if we did), so are constantly surrounded by some level of noise. True silence therefore seems virtually impossible to experience.

Since pure silence is an unattainable ideal, we tend to use the term to mean something a bit less exact – something more realistic. We could say that a 'working silence' is a relational state: we consider it to be silent if it is significantly quieter than what we are used to. I would hazard a guess that most people who pick up this book aren't hankering after actual silence – that is, 'the complete absence of sound'. If we were we could probably buy a decent pair of earplugs for the cost of this book. I think that in fact most of us want something a little more complex and subtle. We want to capture something of the essence of silence.

If we interpret silence like this, then it can be found in such places as the dead of night, the solemnity of a place of worship, the middle of a cornfield or at the end of a speech before the applause.

Silence embodies a much richer place in our imagination than simply the absence of sound. Silence suggests something wholesome, and something special — reverential, sacred even. It's a source of deep power and a special place of stillness, calm and peace.

AURAL OVERLOAD –
AND WHY IT'S BAD FOR US

In our day-to-day lives, most of us are bombarded by sound and visual stimuli. Right now, as I sit writing in my 'quiet room', I can hear: my cat purring on my knee, the builders next door chatting, children arguing downstairs, Lego being rummaged through, someone coughing, a police siren, traffic, my breathing, the tap of the keys on my laptop, a car engine, a phone ringing, footsteps coming up the stairs, sparrows chirping, clothes rustling, children singing, a pneumatic drill, the wind in the leaves, me swallowing, a pigeon cooing, floorboards creaking, a plane overhead, vegetables being chopped, a door slamming, white noise and another car engine.

Over the course of a few minutes these noises come and go. Some are louder than others and obscure the quieter ones. Others are so quiet, or perhaps so familiar, that I only hear them after several minutes of careful listening. Even if we are not fully aware of it, all these sounds can tug at our attention.

There are also the sounds that may not be present at any one particular moment, but that we are listening out for. These potential sounds may be even more distracting. We could be expecting to hear the baby cry, a knock at the door or the beep of a phone. Feeling as though we are about to be interrupted can disrupt our focus, as our thoughts continually wander away from the present moment and onto the anticipated event. Accompanying feelings of irritation cause even more disruption – often far more than the interruption itself.

We live in an age of information and communication, which leads to an abundance of both aural and visual 'noise'. We are so habituated to receiving noise and stimulation that we may feel lonely or bored when there is a lack of it. That's why we turn on the radio when we are driving, exercising or doing DIY, or check our social media feed while we are in a queue at a supermarket. The problem is that because we reach out for stimulation so often, we have ended up in a situation where we can't seem to take a break from it. Society expects us to keep up with the news, our emails, social media, fashion and opinion. If we are not careful, the constant imput can overwhelm us.

In a world of information, where we are inundated by messages and data from all sides, it is survival of the fittest. In order to get heard, messages need to shout louder and flash more brightly, both literally and metaphorically. Companies, charities, institutions and others pump more and more money into their advertising in order to get their messages across. Social media, email and our phones flood us with alerts, texts, statuses and other data from friends, family, colleagues and, of course, businesses. The distinction between public and private has become blurred over social media. We are alerted not only to messages aimed directly at us – conversations between other people also routinely appear in our feed. It can be hard to 'turn away' from discussions that in fact have nothing to do with us. Adverts infiltrate not only our newspapers, transport, buildings and street furniture, but also the websites we visit, our emails and our social media pages. They target us with increasing sophistication as they gather our data. We purposefully set our phones, tablets, watches and other devices with alarms and ringers to alert us when we need to respond or do something.

This is all before we even consider the people around us, such as our colleagues, children and partners, clients and customers, fellow passengers on public transport, shop assistants and passers-by, and friends and acquaintances. We have to navigate countless interactions on a daily basis. This may be especially the case if we live in a densely populated town or city. Our day may involve a seemingly never-ending cycle of conversations, requests, instructions, orders and pleasantries.

Whether we are aware of it or not, we are constantly

sifting through the information overload, sorting the sounds and alerts into the correct categories, and evaluating and prioritising them. The mental energy required to do all this can take a toll; it is a constant drain on our resources, undermining our ability to stay on top of everything. We are like the toddler at an ice-cream counter who cannot choose between the flavours, and is eventually so overwhelmed by the vast choice that he bursts into tears.

The consequence of this proliferation is that we end up suffering from stress. Stress is caused by the 'flight-or-fight' response – it is the body's natural defence mechanism against scary or threatening situations. The body gets us ready for action by setting off a range of different processes, including tensing our muscles, accelerating heart and lung action, increasing blood pressure, putting digestion on hold, and increasing blood flow in some areas and constricting it in others. In the modern world we aren't often in a situation when we need to run away, or to stand and defend ourselves physically. Yet the flight-or-fight response is how the body responds to all perceived threats, including psychological ones. As a result, our bodies go into emergency mode every time we read a shocking headline, can't find our wallet or answer a cold call, or when someone criticises us on social media. In short — it happens a lot.

The problem with this is that our bodies aren't supposed to be going into overdrive so regularly. We can end up with chronic stress. That's bad news, not least because stress is linked to all the major killers — heart and lung diseases, cancer and cirrhosis of the liver. Stress knocks our immune system, making us vulnerable to catching common viruses. It leads to anxiety and depression, and has been shown to reduce our life expectancy. Quite apart from anything else, it doesn't feel very nice.

The good news is that stress isn't inevitable. There are things we can do to help prevent it from happening in the first place, and we can also learn how to let it go when it does arise. Instead of always switching on the flight-or-fight response, we can encourage the body to slip into 'relaxation mode'. Relaxation leads to a decrease in heart and respiration rates, a lowering of blood pressure and a reduction in muscle tension. When we are relaxed we enjoy life more. It feels good. We all know this, so why do we find it so hard to relax? For most people the answer is that there is just too much stuff going on. Silence is a strategy that we can adopt to set things right.

'I don't think ...'

'Then you shouldn't talk,' said the Hatter.

LEWIS CARROLL,

Alice in Wonderland, 1865

WHAT IS THE ART OF SILENCE?

We may recognise that our lives are too busy and too noisy and we need to bring in a little more peace.

Perhaps we want to slow things down, or maybe we just want to learn how to make the best use of the quieter periods that we already have. We look for something of the spirit of silence, because we intuitively know that more of things – more stuff or more stimulation – is not going to lead to greater happiness.

The notion of silence can help us redress the balance of this crazy, chaotic world that we live in. It can give us the space we need to allow our bodies and minds to relax, so that we can become the healthy, wholesome individuals we want to be.

Silence is a strategy for living.

There are three very powerful ways in which we can harness the power of silence and bring more of it into our lives.

Quieting the environment We can make changes to the world around us. We can do this by spending time in quieter places, and by engaging in activities that are conducive to calm. We can think of this as setting the conditions for silence.

Cultivating peaceful relationships The way in which we interact with those around us has a huge impact on the quality of our lives. We can bring peace into our conversations and our way of being with others. This is a way for us to 'act out' our silence.

Nurturing an inner silence By working with the mind, we can learn how to cultivate a sense of inner silence. We can draw from this whatever the circumstances of the moment.

Arranged in three parts, this book explores each of these approaches for bringing more silence into our lives. Within each part there are shorter sections discussing the differing aspects of these ideas. In some places there is practical guidance, while in others the text is more reflective. Dotted around you will also find a collection of visualisations, meditations, quotations, snippets and facts. These have been selected to help you to explore new ways of making contact with silence.

A NOTE ON WORDS

Silence often means the absence of speech or words. You might ask why we would reach for a book – which, inevitably, is full of words – to find silence. It is my hope that the words in this book will act as pointers to the silences that we can achieve. I'm not talking about a mechanical silence – earplugs can help you with that. I mean a broader kind of silence, a slowing down, a lessening of noise and stimulation. Cultivating this kind of silence is a kind of practice in itself. This is what we can call the art of silence. There is a Buddhist saying: 'The finger that points to the moon is not the moon.' The words in this book are not themselves the answer, but they may nudge you in the direction you want to go.

· ·

EXERCISE

Shedding sound

- Sit down with a pen and paper in your hand.
- First of all, write down the loudest sound that you can hear in the next few seconds.
- Now write down the next three loudest sounds.
- Listen further and make a list of every other sound you can hear.
- Can you find 10 more sounds?
- Can you hear the sound of your ears? Listen carefully.
- What do they sound like?

· ·

If we had a keen vision and feeling of
all ordinary human life, it would be like
hearing the grass grow and the squirrel's
heart beat, and we should die of that roar
which lies on the other side of silence.

GEORGE ELIOT,

Middlemarch, 1871

Quieting the environment

In Silence there is eloquence. Stop weaving
and see how the pattern improves.

RUMI, PERSIAN POET,

13th century AD

Searching for silence is not just about lowering the
sound levels around you (though that may be a big part
of it). A movement towards silence can also embody a
more general aspiration to strip away all of the unnec-
essary clutter from your life. That could be in the form
of belongings, workload, media or responsibilities,

because too much of that stuff is leading to stress and overload. Every time we have to deal with something, we are potentially laying ourselves open to the flight-or-fight response. Even if the things are fairly easy to deal with by themselves, when we add them all together they can become overwhelming and stressful. So in this section of the book we'll look at how to tone down the 'noise' in your life.

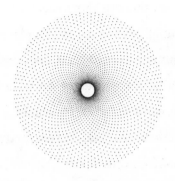

MAKING SPACE FOR SILENCE

Feeling as though we are not on top of things is a major cause of stress. So, why is it that we have so much stuff to do? We only have a set amount of time in each day, and there is a limit to how much we can squeeze into that time – we can only go so fast. Yet so many of us feel as if we are constantly behind. Of course, there is a certain amount that we *have* to do each day. We have to prepare and eat our meals, we may need to care for our children, we need to clean and maintain our home and we probably have work to do. For most of us, it isn't possible or appropriate to simply lie in bed all day doing nothing. However, many of us feel we need to do far more than just the basics of living.

Inevitably, there will be times in our lives when everything will be going faster than we find comfortable, for example when we have a major work deadline, or are building up for a big occasion such as a wedding or house move. At times like these we'll need to draw on our inner reserves rather than try to 'fix' the situation. I talk more about this in part 3. However, if it feels as though you are being dragged along on an intercity train all the time, then you probably need to do something about it. You won't be able to create space and silence if you are constantly on the back foot.

Given that you cannot create more hours, you only really have one option, which is to reduce the number of tasks. Sometimes it can seem utterly impossible to see where you can cut back. You may feel so overloaded that you don't even have time to take a step back and see what can be done. Yet making even the smallest of adjustments can have a major impact on your stress levels. Creating gaps around your tasks (even small ones) allows pockets of silence to filter through to your busy life. So where should you begin?

PRIORITISE WHAT'S IMPORTANT – LOSE WHAT IS NOT

Take some time to think through your week and consider what's really important to you. It might be essentials such as having a shower and taking the dog for a walk, or activities you wish you could make time for, such as baking with the children, reading a book or having a glass of wine with your partner. Are you allowing enough time to do these things, so that you can do them in an unhurried way and take pleasure in them? Or are you just cramming them in between other jobs (if you manage to do them at all, that is)?

If you haven't got time for the things that are important to you, it may be necessary to let go of some of your activities. You may feel so committed to certain activities and projects that giving them up seems impossible. However, taking stock of what you are currently signed up for can help you to work out if you are doing too much. Sometimes we carry on doing things long after we stop enjoying them because we feel guilty about giving them up. There are other things that we do enjoy, but it may be that we are signed up for so many activities that we feel continually rushed.

At times we feel constricted by activities that we have agreed to do on behalf of other people. Parents often spend a lot of time ferrying children around from one activity to the next. Are the children doing too much? Check whether you may have overfilled their timetables, too. Sometimes it can be hard to let go of activities that may have been important at one time but are now not so necessary. For example, if your children take swimming lessons, it may not be necessary for them to have them throughout the year. If you volunteer for a project, perhaps you can take a break at times. Cutting down your activities doesn't mean that you have to abandon them completely. You can just say, 'No, not this time,' or 'Let's see about that in a couple of months.' If you are the type of person who always says yes to things, saying no (or no, not now) can be extremely powerful. Giving up just one job or responsibility can make a big difference to the overall feel of your week.

On a practical level, if you are engaged in fewer activities this literally allows you more time. Instead of immediately filling it with chores or other jobs, you can allow moments of silence to arise in the gaps. Pauses provide opportunities to appreciate and enjoy the activities you do retain, which can be hard when you are rushing from one thing to another.

On a psychological level, starting to say no can represent a switch to a more conscious way of living. When you review your activities and carefully choose which ones to take on or continue, you are fostering a calm, unhurried attitude towards life. Rather than being ruled by circumstances, trying to make do as best you can, you are making a conscious choice. This can contribute to a sense of internal silence and calm, which is discussed in more depth in part 3.

QUESTIONS TO CONSIDER BEFORE SAYING 'YES'

- Is it essential?
- Does it make you happy?
- Does it make you more happy than relaxing at home?
- Does it bring happiness to others?
- Do you have enough time to do it justice?
- Will you be so rushed that you will find it difficult to be calm?
- Is it something you need to do?

REALISTIC EXPECTATIONS ABOUT WHAT YOU 'OUGHT' TO BE DOING

We are bombarded with messages about how we should be living our lives. We are told that we should be having fun in many different ways. Yet the only person who can oversee the whole is you. Check that you don't have unrealistic expectations about how much you can do. You could be left feeling continually disappointed when you don't get to do everything, or may end up perpetually rushed as you try to squeeze everything in.

So, for example, you might nurture a beautiful fantasy of building a tree house with your child, or of indulging in a candle-lit bath. These are lovely things to do, but it's OK for them to be special. You don't have to be doing them every week. Feeling guilty about not fitting in 'quality time' (for yourself or with others) can also contribute to feeling overly committed.

TOO MUCH CHOICE

One factor that contributes to feeling overwhelmed is having too much choice. For a long time advertising has led us to believe that choice is a good thing. We have come to believe that we are entitled to choose pretty much anything – our clothes, holidays, food (regardless of what season it is), cars, music and electronic devices. Yet this proliferation of choice is really very confusing and stressful. Choosing also takes time. Every time we need to make a decision, we spend a bit of mental energy working out what to do (what to eat, cook or watch).

Embracing simplicity is a way to counteract this overabundance. Fewer choices to make also results in less internal chatter from making endless decisions. This is not to say that we should never have any variety – it is the 'spice of life', after all. But spice should be used in small doses. We don't want to ladle out a big bowl of it for every meal. In the meantime, it's fine to keep wearing the same outfit until it needs washing. It's fine to have pasta every Thursday. You don't need to switch to a new shampoo every time it runs out.

Keeping things simple and rejecting over-consumption will bring relief in the short term, but you might also find that it has longer term consequences. Once you reduce the need to keep buying and consuming both goods and experiences, you may find that you don't need to work so hard and earn as much money. You may even find that you can downsize. Perhaps that means working fewer hours, or switching to a job that pays less but fills you with joy. You may find that you want to move to a smaller house, so that you can spend less time organising and tidying your belongings and your home. All these changes can free up more time for space and silence.

· ·

EXERCISE

Write out your timetable

Take a piece of paper and write out a simple timetable of all the jobs that you are involved with each day. Use a highlighter to mark the jobs that are absolutely essential. Use a different-coloured highlighter to mark the ones that bring you real pleasure. See whether you can simplify or prune what is left.

· ·

CLEARING OUT THE CLUTTER

Reducing the amount of physical stuff in your home is one way to simplify your life. If you have rails and rails of clothes, for example, then every time you open your wardrobe you need to make complex choices about what to wear. However, if you have simplified your wardrobe to just a handful of versatile quality items, you will be able to pick out what to wear quickly and confidently. I've noticed that when I don't have any items that I especially like, I tend to over-compensate by having lots of mediocre items – as if the quantity can make up for the lack of quality. It can't.

Much of the clutter that we surround ourselves with represents unfinished jobs or unmade decisions – papers that need filing, unfinished craft projects, DIY jobs left undone, gifts that we never really liked, and odds and sods that we hang on to 'just in case'. The problem with such clutter is that it tugs at us as a kind of visual to-do list. It is a kind of 'noise' that is forever droning on in the background, sapping our attention, and making it hard for us to hear or think clearly.

It is very easy to get sucked into the tide of more-ness. Taking steps to reduce your responsibilities and commitments and to clear your physical space can have a major impact on your quality of life. Having done so, you may find that you now have time in between activities to take a breath. If you have managed to clear some of your clutter, you will hopefully find that your belongings are much easier to keep tidy and well maintained, so that it will be easier to find and use them.

Of course, I have only touched upon some ideas here – the subjects of simplifying your space and your timetable could each warrant a book. The point is that by embracing the idea of simplicity, you can start to get a taste of something that silence can offer you.

Creating a bit more space in our lives isn't really that hard – but we can only do it if we really want it. We may only have time for a few moments on either side of an activity, but if we are not prioritising silence, then those seconds will easily be subsumed by the next job.

However, when we allow silence to slip into the gaps – even if they are very tiny ones – we can use these pauses to come back to the present moment, and to take stock and appreciate what's going on. The more we find ourselves enjoying and making use of silence, the easier it will be for us to incorporate it into our lives.

. . . .

EXERCISE

Build a walk into your weekly routine

Think about a time in your week when you can make space for a walk that is just for pleasure. Go by yourself without any specific purpose in mind. Don't use it as an opportunity to pop to the shops. It doesn't have to be a long walk – perhaps 20–30 minutes, or even 10 minutes if you don't have more time. Make a note of the time you'll be going for the walk in a diary or calendar, and when the time comes for it don't make excuses. Leave your phone at home or switch it to airplane mode, then set off. You may have an idea about your route in advance, but if you do don't be too fixed on it. Use the opportunity to be spontaneous. Walk slowly. You don't need to cover any set distance. Look at what is around you as you go. Be curious about what you might find.

. . . .

REACHING FOR YOUR PHONE

If we don't make a point of safeguarding them, all too often the spaces that we create disappear as soon as we establish them. One of the biggest threats to moments of silence are screens. When we find we have a spare minute, it is all too easy to go and look at a screen and fill that space right back up again.

Nowadays, when we go into a public space such as a train station, college campus or park, it is striking to see how many people are using their phones. Many use their phones as a watch, which means that checking it becomes habitual – a tic, even. The problem is that as well as looking at the time, we check everything else as well. It often seems as if the majority of people have their phones to their ears or held in their palms. Once or twice I have turned around in a seat on a bus and looked back at the passengers – to find that every single one was using their phone.

What would this scene have looked like 20 years ago? I expect that some passengers would have been talking to each other. Some might have been reading a book or newspaper. Others would have been looking ahead or out of the window.

This is not to say that these activities were in some way inherently better than communicating via technology. In many cases our ability to connect has brought about positive change. However, it does seem that today there is a kind of unease about being alone and

33

unoccupied. It's rare to see people truly by themselves. It seems as if we always have to be doing something – and preferably be in contact with someone else. We might tell ourselves that as we are so busy it makes sense to use those 'otherwise wasted' moments to check for messages, but perhaps we really do so because we are afraid of having nothing to do.

What exactly is it that is so terrifying about being unoccupied? We worry that we will get bored – and we have been fed many messages to the effect that boredom is intolerable. But what exactly is boredom? Perhaps it is merely a resistance to experiencing what it is like to be ourselves. So there is a kind of conflict going on for us: on the one hand we are afraid that if we have nothing to do we will be bored; on the other hand we crave some respite from the constant stimulation and demands of society.

We ask ourselves how we can get more silence. Perhaps the truth is that the silence is already there for the taking but we just don't know how to accept it.

Calm soul of all things! make it mine
To feel, amid the city's jar,
That there abides a peace of thine,
Man did not make, and cannot mar!

The will to neither strive nor cry,
The power to feel with others give!
Calm, calm me more! nor let me die
Before I have begun to live.

MATTHEW ARNOLD,
'Lines Written in Kensington Gardens', 1849

For many of us, checking our messages has become something of an addiction. It might be the first thing you do when you wake up – perhaps you keep your phone by the side of your bed. Leaving your phone at a friend's home causes major consternation, and if you should happen to drop it in a puddle or have it stolen, you may experience an extraordinary amount of stress.

We rely on our phones to such a high degree that suggesting that we simply cut back on using them is pretty pointless. It might be rude and unproductive to leave messages unanswered, and your work could suffer. However, I do think that we can bring in a bit of discipline around our messages. If you always reply immediately to every message, people will come to expect that of you and you will never be able to switch off.

Only you will be able to say what level of phone use is right for you. Some people I know always keep their phone in their work bag or even in their car. Others have it with them in a pocket (or out on a table) at all times. If you find yourself constantly checking your phone, perhaps a rough rule of thumb (such as putting it away before dinner) might help to protect some of your evenings and give you time for quiet moments.

Even if you feel as though you are just responding to other people's messages, do check how much you are feeding the communications explosion. Last year I went on a retreat for 10 days – no mobiles allowed. When

I came off the retreat I turned on my phone and, as expected, several hundred messages pinged through. As I scrolled through them, however, I noticed that the majority were sent in the first couple of days. Towards the end of my time away the messages tailed off. This taught me a good lesson: many of the messages I receive are generated by me. If I stop sending messages it doesn't take long for the incoming ones to dry up, too.

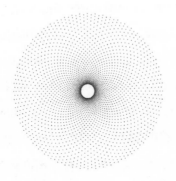

KEEPING OURSELVES
OCCUPIED WITH
WHOLESOME ACTIVITIES

If we want to make more time for silence, we have to recognise that continually checking our devices prevents us from welcoming silence into our lives. Without really thinking about it, when we needlessly check our social media feed we are rejecting silence.

That also means rejecting the benefits that silence can bring – the opportunity to relax, moments for appreciation, and time to take stock, find balance and renew ourselves. So how do we go about weaning ourselves off our devices? One way is to be very strict with ourselves about not continually checking and sending messages. Another way is to make an effort to fill our time with more wholesome, calming activities.

Of course, I'm not advocating that you suddenly sign up for a zillion activities and cram your timetable unrealistically full. However, I do suggest that you should try to make wholesome, healthy choices from time to time when you are deciding what to do. So, for example, instead of trawling through shopping sites for the next purchase, put that on hold and choose an activity that will nourish you.

SPENDING TIME IN NATURE

Natural areas are really good places to start cultivating the essence of silence. By spending time in nature we are creating space away from all the demands of modern life: we are literally squeezing the stimulation out of the timetable. By practising relaxation we are also strengthening that inner place of silence. That's why we continue to feel relaxed when we return to work after a walk in a park – at least for a spell, anyway. Although we may dream of relaxing on a beach on a desert island or on a lazy river bank, perhaps we don't need to look that far. It could be that the importance we attach to exotic destinations or rural retreats is in fact an excuse to avoid looking for nature and solitude nearby.

. . . .

EXERCISE

A neighbouring tree

Wherever you are right now, take a moment to look around you and consider: where is the nearest tree? When you can, go to visit the tree. If it is in a space that is inaccessible to you, for example in a neighbour's garden, choose another tree that you can reach. Get to know the tree.

Place your hand on the bark and feel the texture under your fingers. Is it smooth or rough? Smell the bark. Do any particles come away in your fingers? What about the branches? How are they shaped? Are they thick or thin, or strong or spindly? Can you see marks of pruning or other damage on the tree? Is it in leaf? What are the leaves like (or the lack of leaves, if there are none). Are the leaves newly opened, or coming to the end of their lifespan? What colours can you find in the leaves? Gently finger the leaves near your ear – how do they sound?

As you stand next to the tree, breathe. Consider how oxygen and carbon dioxide are exchanged between you. Look at the ground. Notice how the roots of the tree enter the earth and bind the tree in place, holding it steady and still, and also sustaining it. Consider how eventually all parts of our bodies pass into the earth – hair and skin cells that we constantly shed during our lives, and eventually the rest of our bodies after we die.

. . . .

When we stop and take the time to look, most of us find that nature is close at hand. There may not be a sweeping moorland or craggy mountaintop nearby, but even in the busiest cities we can find parks, wooded walks, gardens and scrubby patches of wilderness.

It may be that the green spaces near you have been designed by town planners and are carefully tended and guarded. Perhaps nature has reclaimed a vacant spot nearby – a derelict yard, perhaps, or a disused railway line. How often do we take the time to pass through such patches of nature? What about pausing while among the greenery – perhaps sitting among the grasses or standing in the trees? It could be that a small alteration to your normal route to the shops or a bus stop could take you through a 'wilder' path. Or you may already pass through green areas but don't really take the time to notice them.

There is a river flowing through the part of the city where I live, and some areas of marshland lie nearby. A very well-used footpath leads to the city centre. It traverses a marsh, then continues over a footbridge across the river, and is punctuated by old-fashioned lamp posts. I regularly walk and cycle down this path, along with thousands of other commuters. Not long ago I happened to be walking on another footpath that runs nearby. From there I could see the many cyclists and pedestrians walking along the main path. However, the reeds of the marsh obscured the concrete underfoot. The golden afternoon sunlight was shining behind the people in such a way that they appeared to me as silhouettes. As I observed the line of figures moving along the path, some going in one direction, some in the other, I was suddenly struck by a notion that the scene could have been from 150 years ago – the marsh itself was timeless, and the old-fashioned lamp posts lent it a Victorian air.

When we pause and look on a scene with fresh eyes, something can be opened up to us and the scene may look startlingly different – even when it is very familiar. This particular section of path near my house happens to be rather evocative. Much of the time the path is simply a drag – a monotonous stretch that has to be got through on the way to somewhere else. At other times, especially if the floodwaters are unusually high, or if a mist is hanging over the reeds or the hawthorn in the hedges has just blossomed – that is if I am nudged to look at it more carefully for some reason – I am struck by its simple beauty. It is at times like this that I realise how much there is to see, if only we take the time to look.

> There is a pleasure in the pathless woods,
> There is a rapture on the lonely shore,
> There is society where none intrudes,
> By the deep Sea, and music in its roar:
> I love not Man the less, but Nature more,
>
> LORD BYRON,
> *Childe Harold's Pilgrimage*, 1812–18

OPEN-ACCESS WOODS

Going out and enjoying nature is beneficial for all of us. We recognise that 'fresh air' is pleasant, refreshing and rejuvenating. We enjoy being outside. This is especially the case when we have gone outside on purpose to appreciate the offerings of the natural world – by going for a walk or to sunbathe in the garden, for example.

We all know that it is good for children to play outside – and it's not just because it allows us to get them out from under our feet. Educators increasingly understand the importance of the outdoors for children, and lately nature play has been formally introduced into the curriculum in many mainstream schools through the Forest School programme. Forest School operates on the philosophy that if children are given free rein to play in a self-directed way in an enriching natural environment – like that offered by a woodland – they will naturally develop their confidence, which can boost their achievements in all areas.

Spending time outside can be done without any formal structure, whatever age you are. Forest School goes a long way to prove the benefit of nature play for children in an increasingly indoor and technological world. It is a way of safeguarding that precious resource. However, we don't need formal qualifications or a special time slot to go outside. It is important that people don't feel that they can't go out without some form of training.

In the same way that children don't need to be in Forest School to go out and play, adults don't need to participate in any grand or complicated activity to get outdoors either. A hiking expedition or canoe trip can provide a wonderful experience, but we can access the outdoors in a much more simple, low-key way. We can simply go outside. That could be for leisure, or it could mean taking our ordinary indoor work outdoors.

Because so many of us work in offices and other indoor environments, being outdoors often signifies leisure and relaxation – the outdoors is an obvious place for us to look for more silence. However, we don't have to sit outside doing nothing in order to take advantage of the natural peace found in nature. Activities such as gardening, drawing and painting, playing with children and DIY can (and in some cases must) be done outside. Sometimes these activities feel like work – at other times they are purely part of leisure. In either case, being outside and appreciating the silence inherent in nature can help us bring the quality of enjoyment to the work.

Of course, nature is rarely (if ever) technically silent. In fact, it is likely to be quieter indoors than outside. But the 'noise' of nature is normally the kind of noise that doesn't make demands on us. The wind, the birds, the movement of water – all of these are the sounds of the world working in harmony already. We don't need to do anything about them or to have an opinion on them. As discussed later, with the right frame of mind even man-made noises such as those produced by construction work, traffic and aircraft don't necessarily need to detract from the sense of silence. As long as they don't directly affect us or require us to do anything, there is no need for us to view them differently from, say, the birds going about their business.

. . . .

VISUALISATION

Under the willow tree

Imagine you are walking through a meadow. A golden breeze carries insects and seed-flecks above the wildflowers, wings catching the light. You know where you are going but you do not rush. You can see the place up ahead – that tussock of grass beneath the tree. Your feet carve a path through the grasses, swish-swishing to let you pass. Crickets leap out of the way and renew their sawing elsewhere.

Now you are closer. You can see the river beyond the grassy bank. More insects dart above the smooth sheet of darkness, and a red-faced moorhen, startled by your presence, springs into the water and ripples the surface. You have been here before. The grass is warm, dry and springy: it cradles you as you sit.

You take off your shoes and tuck your socks inside them. The grasses tickle the soles of your feet. Now you stretch and lie back. A willow tree reaches overhead, shading you with its dappled light. The sky speckles blue between the green-golden leaves and more seed-heads drift above you, sometimes floating as if suspended in mid-air, sometimes caught in invisible eddies, as dragonflies and greenflies disturb the air.

You close your eyes and the faint smell of warm mud curls into your nostrils. Grass stems prick into your arms as you fold them under your head. You hear the trickle of the water as it heads steadily seawards. The buzz and whirr of insects – it's been there all along, but you allow it to fill your ears until you can't hear anything else. And now you let that sound fade as the gentle rustle of the breeze in the leaves takes centre stage.

The muscles in your limbs begin to loosen. The ground seems to reach up to support the length of your body, gently holding it, and you seem to sink further into the grasses. Your breath, now smooth and easy, lengthens.

You lie here for some time – listening.

. . . .

NOURISHING PASTIMES

Going out into nature is not the only way to bring more silence into our lives. Other activities may benefit us just as well or more. Different people find fulfilment in different ways, but it is often the case that an activity which involves quiet, focused attention can bring us a lot of satisfaction. Some people particularly enjoy activities such as crafts and playing musical instruments, which also involve handiwork and combine elements of both skill and creativity.

Hobbies such as knitting, woodwork, painting, baking and gardening can be wonderful for making time for quiet, calm activity. By directing our attention to these pursuits, we are earmarking time for quiet concentration. If you have a busy family life, you may not have much time to devote to your favourite activities. However, you can bring this element of quiet calm into other activities. In fact, the activities do not have to be technically 'quiet' in order for you to bring in the essence of silence. Perhaps you can join your children in a rather boisterous game of stuck in the mud. It may not be quiet, yet by joining in wholeheartedly, without your mind half on other tasks, you may capture something of the spirit of simplicity and silence.

Other people find that sport (see also page 61) provides the way to renewing their spirit. Sport involves the element of focus and also some degree of challenge. Some sports are certainly not calm and quiet, but because we may become fully absorbed in them, they still have the effect of quieting and refreshing our minds.

All of these activities have in common the fact that we become absorbed in them. While we are doing them, we forget ourselves and other distractions; our minds become focused and alert. Some people refer to this as a state of 'flow'. Activities that present a certain amount of challenge and require us to hone a skill to meet that challenge are the most likely to keep us engaged. Although this is perhaps not silence in the strictest sense, by keeping our minds on just one wholesome activity, we are preventing ourselves from being drawn into a series of other competing noisy tasks and thoughts.

> Rest is not idleness, and to lie sometimes
> on the grass under trees on a summer's day,
> listening to the murmur of the water, or
> watching the clouds float across the sky, is
> by no means a waste of time.
>
> JOHN LUBBOCK,
> *The Use of Life*, 1894

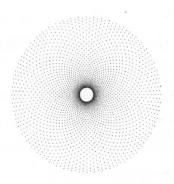

SEARCHING SPACES
FOR SOLITUDE

We have looked at how spending time in nature can help us in our quest for silence. Our physical environment can have a massive effect on the way we feel and behave. It can be just small details such as whether or not there is a window open that contribute to this effect — or occurrences on a much grander scale.

Throughout history, humans have gone to the edges of the Earth in order to explore the limits of their environment. A quest for the extremes often involves turning your back on societal comforts and venturing into new realms where silence represents the unknown. In the silent spaces at the edges of the world, we let go of the usual structures and framework of civilisation. At the same time as pushing at the natural frontiers – in the depths of the ocean, up mountains and across deserts – explorers have tested not only their physical abilities, but also their mental endurance. Travelling to the extremes in the physical world also makes huge psychological demands as we leave the familiar and forge new pathways.

In many societies, journeying has long been a tradition to mark the passage from youth to adulthood. Australian Aborigines traditionally kept the practice of walkabout, which is when adolescent men spent several weeks or months in the Outback learning about the land of their ancestors. Similar journeys and rites of passage can be found among Native Americans and other tribespeople.

Wanderlust seems to be common to all peoples, yet in our modern civilised world it is hard to find an outlet for adventure. Western teenagers may try to sate the desire to journey by travelling in 'gap years' between school and college, or during their holiday breaks. However, because of the ubiquity of the Internet and mobile phones, travel does not involve quite the same level of 'going away' and switching off as it used to. It is hard to find silence. Travellers (especially young ones) are expected to stay in much closer contact with their families and friends back at home. Through social media, conversations can continue even when friends are on opposite sides of the world. The practicalities of independent travel have been made vastly easier through information such as online timetables and hostel-booking websites. Not so long ago, backpackers relied on guidebooks, word-of-mouth recommendations and a fair bit of luck to successfully navigate foreign infrastructures. Nowadays, travellers can plan and book whole itineraries before setting off on their travels. If they need to alter arrangements on-the-go, then WiFi is readily available. Thus the clear advantages of modern technology have also resulted in something of the spirit of adventure being lost.

All this means that those who seek solitude and silence must make much more effort and go to more extremes to find the 'wild places'. Seeking silence is not just about finding a place with a low noise level – it may also be about moving beyond our usual social infrastructures. Going to places that are notable for their absence of society can force us to reassess how we interact with society. It is only when our lives are stripped back to a more basic level that we can start to see what kinds of assumptions we make on a daily level – many of which we have no idea that we hold.

Venturing into the unknown does not necessarily have to involve months of journeying into the wilderness. In fact, it is possible for people to access otherworldly, silent spaces much more quickly, though perhaps in equally extreme ways. Leisure pursuits and exercise – and in particular the more extreme sports – can offer us a chance to step outside the normal bounds of existence.

> A man can be himself only so long as he is
> alone; and if he does not love solitude, he
> will not love freedom; for it is only when he
> is alone that he is really free.

ARTHUR SCHOPENHAUER,
Essays and Aphorisms, 1851

UNDER THE SEA

People have been diving underneath the sea for as long as we know. Divers have hunted for pearls for thousands of years – the oldest known natural pearl was found on a Neolithic site in the United Arab Emirates and is around 7,500 years old. From the writings of Homer and Plato, we know that sponge diving was popular in Ancient Greek times, and it still continues to this day. Of course, people have dived to hunt fish and harvest seaweed throughout history.

Alongside this functional diving, people have dived and swum for pleasure. For many people the attraction of diving is that it provides the chance to 'get away from it all'. Quite apart from the wonders that the seas have to offer, they are also special for what the watery world excludes – there's no electricity, no phones, no Internet, no talking . . .

Divers must forego conversation during the sport, and instead focus on interacting with the natural world around them. This is an incredibly refreshing change of pace from everyday life for most. Although it is often referred to as the 'silent world', in actual fact the sea is anything but silent. Diving birds, crashing waves, rain, lava flowing into the sea – there are many diverse causes of sound beneath the seas. It is estimated that more than 500 fish species make some kind of sound. However, many of the sounds are of such a low frequency that the unaided human ear cannot detect them.

> On the surface of the ocean, men wage war
> and destroy each other; but down here, just
> a few feet beneath the surface, there is a
> calm and peace, unmolested by man.
>
> JULES VERNE,
> *Twenty Thousand Leagues Under*
> *the Sea*, 1870

OTHER SPORTS

Diving is perhaps unique because the nature of the environment prohibits talk. Yet most sports have similar elements. Often the enjoyment of physical pursuits comes from sensations in the body, and a refreshed and perhaps alternative way of looking at the world. Most sports include a degree of focused concentration, where we direct our minds and bodies towards a single aim. As already mentioned, this has the effect of excluding many noisy distractions – both internal and external.

An interesting thing about sport is that it also tends to take us to a particular physical space, be it outdoors or in a purpose-built environment. However, the point is that when we set out to take part in a sport, we have to make a commitment to the activity, whether that's going to a certain place, wearing the right clothes or bringing equipment. Once we have made this commitment, it is easier to stick to the task at hand and avoid the usual interruptions and distractions of everyday life. While we may not ordinarily think of sport as being silent, in fact the state of focused attention on one activity contains much of the essence of silence. For some people, this makes sport a useful route towards achieving more peace and calm.

SPACE TRAVEL

If the mysteries of the sea capture our collective imagination, then space travel is perhaps the ultimate frontier. Humans have gazed up at the stars for millennia – and wondered. The Moon is the epitome of that silent, lonely, unreachable place, and has long been the muse for poets, philosophers and artists.

With the Space Race and Neil Armstong walking on the Moon in 1969, space travel finally became a reality (albeit for a limited few). The quest to put people into space and on the Moon was a political strategy, yet it tapped into our innate desire to explore and push at boundaries. 'Being an astronaut' became the top career ambition for many children over the following decades.

What is it about the Moon and space travel that so captivates us? Space represents a vastness so immense that it is incomprehensible to us. There is something about turning our mind to this enormity that sets off a process within us. The very idea of space seems to stretch our minds in some way, so that we are more willing to be open to what it offers.

Of course, most of us will never experience space travel, but we can still explore its qualities through literature, art and our own imaginations. Space represents a silence that is both immense and boundless. We can make a connection with it through playful visualisation.

. . . .

VISUALISATION

Watching the Moon

Imagine you are sitting on the grass, looking up into a cool sky. The darkness is pricked with stars. There is a glow in the distance, and some low pale clouds drift over the dark hills. As you watch, a sliver of light breaks above the horizon and slowly a coin of silver rises above it.

You gaze into the shining Moon and its round face gazes back down at you. As you watch, the Moon seems to grow – a swelling disc that takes up more of the sky. It expands until you can clearly see the craters and mountains that rumple its surface. Your eyes are fixed on the Moon, and you vaguely notice that the rest of the sky has disappeared.

Now you realise that you are rising up off the ground and travelling towards the Moon. It is as if you are being pulled along an unseen cable. First your chest goes up, and slowly, without any effort, your legs unfold and you are drawn up on to your feet. Your body continues to rise as your heels, and now your toes, have lifted off from the grass. You feel extremely light.

The Moon is now so large and so bright that you can see nothing else. The light envelops you. It is not a hot light, but a comfortable bright coolness. You seem to be moving directly into the centre of the light, until it is all around you – in front, behind, to the left, to the right, above and below. You are inside the Moon and it is inside you.

. . . .

SECLUSION AS A LIFE CHOICE

Remote places are not just for sport, adventure, or political or commercial gain. Since ancient times there have been people seeking out places of seclusion in order to explore deeper within themselves. These people are not thrill seekers, but their quests may be equally if not more challenging and extreme. They travel to remote places not so much for what these places can offer in themselves but more for what they are not.

Humanity has a long history of cave dwelling. Cave paintings and other artefacts show us that caves provided shelter for the earliest humans. In more recent times caves have been the places of seclusion, into which people have withdrawn from society in order to explore deeper into their own minds. All spiritual paths seem to have traditions of devotees retreating into places of hermitage so that they can avoid external distractions.

A modern-day hermit

Tenzin Palmo is a Tibetan Buddhist nun who lived in a cave in the Himalayas for 12 years. She was born in 1943 in Hertfordshire, England, and travelled to India to study Buddhism at the age of 20. After spending 6 years living as the sole nun among 100 monks, Palmo decided, with the permission of her teacher, to retreat to a cave in the remote Lahaul area of India. There she lived in extreme hardship – growing her own sparse food on the side of the mountain and enduring 6–8 months of ice and snow. For 3 of those years she lived in strict meditation retreat, in complete silence and isolation. Some supplies were delivered twice yearly – though at times they failed to arrive.

It may initially seem hard to recognise the benefit of foregoing all creature comforts, company, and even sometimes the basic necessities of food and warmth. Some might consider it to be a kind of masochistic undertaking – one that would be more harmful than helpful. We may find it even harder to see what benefit such strict silence and solitude can bring to others. In fact, going into hermitage is often thought of as a somewhat selfish act, with the idea that withdrawing from society equates to 'turning one's back' on it. Palmo (like many hermits) relied entirely on the charity of others (many of whom had a low income themselves) to support her, so the act of hermitage could even be seen as a burden.

However, the role of the hermit is not only about the hermit's own spiritual path and self-development. The actions of a hermit also have an effect on the wider collective. The hermit who has made phenomenal sacrifices and undergoes extreme personal silence in order to devote their lives to spirituality serves as an inspiration to others. Hermits and monastics can be seen to some extent to be working on our behalf. We cannot all take this path of solitude, but the fact that some of us do reflects on the wider group. This is why communities around hermits (in the East, at least) are glad to support them with gifts of food and other necessities. Hermits are imagined as beacons shining out in the mountains and lighting up the world with their light.

During their silent days, without the distraction of society, many hermits dedicate much of their time to praying and meditating on behalf of others, and actively working on their own capacity to be compassionate. For many people, the idea that hermits are praying for or holding others in mind during meditation can be accepted as being inherently beneficial for the world. Others are more sceptical of the worth of this for others. Yet even the most cynical can understand that a hermit's own personal development will benefit society when (or if) they eventually do return to civilisation. After leaving her cave Palmo dedicated her life to fundraising for a new nunnery, which she founded in 2000. She is now an important advocate for female practitioners of Tibetan Buddhism, who are denied full ordination and have limited rights compared with their male counterparts.

According to spiritual traditions that support the idea of hermitage, practising loving kindness and compassionate prayer has a value in its own right, regardless of whether the practitioner directly applies that compassion in the world. Through their silence and solitude, hermits are learning how to be in the world without causing harm to themselves or others. This ability is of profound importance. People like this, who manage to live in harmony with the world, provide us with a very important role model and are a guiding inspiration. I explore this idea further later (see page 90).

> I find it wholesome to be alone the greater
> part of the time. To be in company, even
> with the best, is soon wearisome and
> dissipating. I love to be alone. I never found
> the companion that was so companionable
> as solitude.

HENRY DAVID THOREAU,

Walden, 1854

Shorter retreats

Spending years in a cave is not for everyone. For those who wish to make a smaller (yet still significant) commitment to the pursuit of silence, retreat centres can offer this opportunity. These are places where people can come to meditate together, often in silence, for a period of a few days or sometimes longer. Participants agree to cut contact with the outside world for the duration of the retreat. Retreat centres may offer courses that are open to everyone, including beginners, or they may run weeks for more experienced meditators.

Retreat centres are often located in remote rural locations far removed from the hustle and bustle of everyday life, but they can also be found in or near towns and cities. Although a remote location may facilitate the feeling of removal from everyday life, in fact the attitude of the meditator is far more important than the location. Going on a meditation retreat can be a profound and life-changing experience, as it gives us the chance to experience silence in an intense and ongoing way.

Other methods of seclusion

There are ways to get a taste of these more extreme kinds of silence right within the midst of our modern lives.

The anechoic chamber Perhaps the closest that we can get to a technical silence is inside an anechoic chamber. This is a room that is completely soundproofed from outside noise. Typically, anechoic chambers have twin walls of steel and 1ft of concrete. Inside, the walls, ceiling and floor are covered with 3ft acoustic wedges that absorb all reverberation. The chambers are used for experiments and tests involving sound. Anechoic means without echo. When a balloon pops inside an anechoic chamber, it sounds more like a 'click' than the big bang that we are familiar with.

Because there are no other noises, people inside the chamber can clearly hear the noises of their bodies.

There are the noises that one would expect, such as the heartbeat and the breath, but also the less familiar functions, such as blood swishing through veins around the ears, and the sounds of muscles contracting in the face and the scalp scraping against the skull. It seems that while we still have ears to hear with, we can never be in absolute silence.

Visitors to anechoic chambers have reported that being able to hear these noises for the first time can give rise to a heightened sense of awareness. They find themselves listening intently to systems and processes of the body to which they had previously never given any thought. The lack of other noise facilitates intro-spection – with all other noises stripped away, the visitor is free to focus their attention on their present experience.

However, some people have found that the noiseless-ness and lack of reverberation is disorientating. Some have even experienced aural hallucinations as their minds tried to compensate for the lack of noise.

Prisoner's cinema The connection between sensory deprivation and hallucinations has been known since long before the development of anechoic chambers. Prisoners who have been kept in solitary confinement in the dark report the phenomenon of the 'prisoner's cinema'. This is where visions of light appear in the darkness – sometimes forming shapes and even realistic images and figures. Some paleoanthropologists have made a connection between the patterns that can emerge in these lights and Paleolithic cave paintings.

The phenomenon has a long tradition in the East, where Tibetan Buddhist monastics have traditionally entered into dark retreats. The retreats, which may last seven weeks or much longer, are only permitted for those who already have considerable spiritual attainment. There is a real danger of becoming detached from reality and slipping into psychosis with this method.

The concept of dark retreats as a therapy is growing in popularity in the West, and a number of organisations offer stays in purpose-built accommodation. The suites are arranged so that the user can feel their way around the room, eat, use the bathroom and sleep, all in pitch darkness. Some therapists claim that their dark retreats can cure ailments ranging from fatigue and stress to eczema. Others emphasise the more spiritual nature of the retreats, and even suggest that 'astral travel' and out-of-body experiences can be accessed.

Floating in space If seven days in total darkness seems too much, flotation tanks offer a rather more scaled-down version. Flotation tanks are widely available in spas and holistic therapy clinics. Users normally spend an hour inside the tank, and the experience is relatively inexpensive. Flotation tanks are filled with water containing enough Epsom salt to cause the users to float. Because the water and air match the body's temperature, after a while it becomes hard to tell where the skin ends and air or water begins. The pod is also darkened and soundproofed, so that the experiences combine for the ultimate in sense deprivation. In order to achieve a similar effect in your own bathtub, you would need about 65lb of salt.

I care for myself. The more solitary, the
more friendless, the more unsustained I am,
the more I will respect myself.

CHARLOTTE BRONTË,
Jane Eyre, 1847

White noise This might at first seem like the antithesis of silence. It is a technical term used in physics that refers to a noise containing multiple frequencies across the whole hearing range, all at equal intensity. This arrangement of sound is heard as a constant buzzing, hissing or 'sh–' sound. Although it may seem to be the last thing that is wanted by silence seekers, in fact white noise is often used as an antidote to other bothersome noises. White-noise machines are marketed as a solution to background noise in the office, as an aid to sleep and even as a method of drowning out tinnitus, or ringing in the ears (which itself is often caused by over-exposure to noise).

White noise is also used by parents trying to help their newborn babies get to sleep. There are numerous websites, videos and apps that play continuous white noise for this purpose. Another way to create 'white noise' is to detune an FM radio and leave it playing static. The theory is that babies are used to hearing the 'whooshing' sounds of blood pumping through the placenta and other biological noises from their life in the womb, so a lack of noise may be unnerving for infants. White noise – or the sound of other droning or rhythmic noises such as those produced by washing machines, vacuum cleaners and showers – can calm babies and help them to stay asleep. Of course, perhaps the most time honoured of these methods is the simple whispering of 'sh-sh-' to help soothe a fractious baby.

It seems that we are drawn to this type of noise, whether it's a uniform white noise produced by an app or machine, or a more natural sound such as waves drawing through pebbles on a beach, or the constant trickle of a mountain stream. I would hazard a guess that these sounds are calming precisely because they are so reliable and repetitive. After a period of time we learn to trust the sound – we know that nothing unexpected is going to happen, so in time we relax and stop listening out for surprises. Pleasant variations in the sound, like those we might hear from waves on a beach or wind through trees, do not disturb us as long as they remain within the expected range. Perhaps they evoke a sense of reassurance and safety, learnt from our time in the womb.

IN SUMMARY

This part of the book has looked at the practical ways of introducing more silence into our lives. We have looked at two main approaches for doing this – making time for silence and going to silent places – both of which can help us to find more silence.

Making time for silence means recognising the value of opening up gaps in our timetables. Allowing pauses to seep into our lives gives us space to reflect. By doing less, we can make much more of the activities that we continue with. If we allow time to take stock and refresh ourselves, we become more aware of our present-moment experiences and can take more joy in life, instead of madly rushing from one activity to another.

The second approach involves consciously looking out for ways to spend time in quieter environments. Some of the examples discussed, such as living in a cave or visiting an anechoic chamber, may not be obvious or likely choices. I have included these more extreme ideas in order to provoke thought. When we become more conscious about the surroundings we choose to spend time in, we can start to make wiser choices about the way in which we live. In many cases the environment we choose to be in will have a major effect on the activities we carry out there, and the way in which we think and behave. Choosing to be in a more peaceful environment can help us to foster a sense of peace and silence within ourselves.

Cultivating peaceful relationships

If you can sit in silence with a person for half an hour and yet be entirely comfortable, you and that person can be friends. If you cannot, friends you'll never be and you need not waste time in trying.

L. M. MONTGOMERY,

The Blue Castle, 1926

It may seem counterintuitive to spend time thinking about words and speech in our quest for silence. Yet conversations can create and define our relationships, which makes them incredibly important. The quality of our speech, and the way we listen and are listened to, are intimately connected to the way we experience silence. If we cannot cultivate peaceful relationships, we will not be able to find peace within ourselves. Let's look at how we can foster peaceful relationships – both by using words and when there is an absence of words.

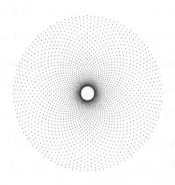

STRATEGIES FOR
SPEAKING KINDLY

Silence is not always a positive state. We have probably all been in situations where anger has resulted in us turning away from others. When we feel hurt or wounded, we try to protect ourselves by disconnecting from other people. It can feel deeply painful to be in this situation. A part of us longs to reconnect, but our anger builds a wall around us and pushes others away. We become locked in our own tower of isolation. When others act like this towards us it can be very difficult to break through to them. When children do it we say that they are sulking – adults we may class as bitter or resentful. Once communication breaks down in this way, silence can become a hostile state – a way of punishing other people.

Clearly, this is not the type of silence that we are aiming for. A silence that brings calm and peace is one that grows out of a base of connectedness, so in order to achieve the kind of silence that we want we first need to work at the way we speak and relate to those around us.

KIND WORDS

Speaking kindly and respectfully to those around us seems like common sense, but it's not always easy to do. If we are not careful with our words it can be easy to react in a knee-jerk style to challenging situations. If, however, we keep trying to speak more kindly, we can become better practised at it. Just making a commitment to speaking thoughtfully can bring about a lot of change. Silence can be a useful friend in trying to improve the quality of our speech. Pauses during conversations give us a chance to breathe and notice our immediate feelings. We can use pauses to 'check in' both with ourselves and with the other person in a conversation.

Why do we sometimes say unhelpful things?

When communicating with another person we sometimes start articulating without really making a decision to talk, and say the first thing that comes into our head without using any kind of filter. That's fine if we are feeling calm and good natured towards the person we are communicating with. If, though, the situation has stirred up some negative feeling from the past (whether recent or not) and we become upset or aggravated, we may find ourselves reverting to 'script'. This is when we blurt out an answer, as if we were saying lines from a play. It may be just the tone or inflection that comes out automatically, or we might parrot the exact words we remember hearing as a child, or what we read in the paper or heard a friend say last week. Such words may be ill judged and unhelpful in the current situation. The person we are speaking to may also react by speaking hastily. This causes the situation to escalate, and everyone may say something they later regret.

Silence can help us to reflect before we speak. It doesn't have to be a lengthy silence – sometimes a momentary pause gives us enough time to note how we are feeling, and to not necessarily let those feelings dictate the tone and content of our speech. At times we may notice too late that we have already started speaking 'script'. We may even catch the tone of our own voice and recognise that it sounds like something from a soap opera. Feeling that we are on a stage is an indication that we may not be responding authentically.

Making a commitment to speaking kindly is not a new idea. Many religions and philosophies espouse rules for helpful speech. There is even a Victorian guide to speech in a poem.

Is It True? Is It Necessary? Is It Kind?

Oh! Stay, dear child, one moment stay,

Before a word you speak,

That can do harm in any way

To the poor, or to the weak;

And never say of any one

What you'd not have said of you,

Ere you ask yourself the question,

'Is the accusation true?'

And if 'tis true, for I suppose

You would not tell a lie;

Before the failings you expose

Of friend or enemy:

Yet even then be careful, very;

Pause and your words well weigh,

And ask if it be necessary,

What you're about to say.

And should it necessary be,

At least you deem it so,

Yet speak not unadvisedly

Of friend or even foe,

Till in your secret soul you seek

For some excuse to find;

And ere the thoughtless word you speak,

Ask yourself, 'Is it kind?'

When you have ask'd these questions three–

True–Necessary–Kind–

Ask'd them in all sincerity,

I think that you will find,

It is not hardship to obey

The command of our Blessed Lord,–

No ill of any man to say;

No, not a single word.

MARY ANN PIETZKER,

Miscellaneous Poems, 1872

Silence and non-harm

Although a hostile silence can be uncomfortable and unhelpful, we have to bear in mind that sometimes it's better not to speak than to say something damaging. We may remember a rule from childhood to the effect that if you can't say anything kind, don't say anything at all.

It's interesting to think of silence in the context of a wider policy of non-harm. What do I mean by non-harm? As a code of behaviour non-harm doesn't get a huge amount of attention. You won't get a certificate for not doing something bad. It may seem that not harming is less important than solving problems and doing good, but in fact not adding more difficulties to this world can be very significant and powerful. This links back to our discussion earlier (see page 41), where we looked at how adding more wholesome activities such as being in nature can redress the balance in our timetables, and squeeze out the more draining, noisesome activities. Non-harm is another way of thinking about silence – it's about not adding any extra agitating or troubling actions to our lives.

When spiritual practitioners make the decision to go into long silent retreats or even into caves, for example in a hermitage, they are practising the idea of non-harm in a very obvious and extreme way (see pages 67–9). However, we can also take this practice of non-harm down to a very subtle level – even to our conversations with our friends and family. Perhaps the most surprising thing about non-harm is that it is very empowering. It's easy to feel disheartened and ineffective when we hear about troubles in the world. However, when we undertake not to add to these or other troubles, even in the smallest way, we are taking full responsibility for ourselves. We are doing what we can.

This is not to say that non-harm should be mistaken for passivity or inaction, because sometimes not acting can cause more harm.

The cruelest lies are often told in silence.

ROBERT LOUIS STEVENSON,

Virginibus Puerisque and Other Papers, 1881

As our interactions with others become ever more complex, we will sometimes need to break out of silence in order to continue to practise non-harm. An overarching policy of silence is not the same as passively accepting injustice. This would be simplistic and unhelpful. Speaking out when we witness wrong-doing is both appropriate and our duty as citizens of the world. The point is that we must use our silence to correctly understand the situation. It is our egos that must be silenced, so that when we do act or speak out we are doing it wisely and with kindness, not out of anger or hatred.

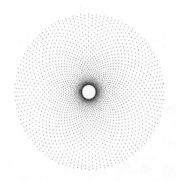

LISTENING AND
BEING HEARD

Listening and being heard are intimately connected to the concept of silence. In this case, silence becomes a receptive state. Listening is not just about hearing what another person is saying.

So often in conversation, instead of listening we are waiting for the other person to finish speaking so that we can jump in with our own ideas. We hold our own opinion steadfast and quickly assess their ideas to see how well they match ours. Or, regardless of what ideas they might have, we use their remarks as a springboard to launch our own opinion.

> 'Yes . . . but what about the impact on the pound?'

> 'That may be true, but you haven't considered the effect on rainforest biodiversity.'

> 'No, you've got it completely wrong.'

> 'I totally agree.'

All of these remarks suggest that the speaker is fixed in their own view, and is not really listening for the purpose of understanding what the other thinks. Even the final comment, 'I totally agree,' indicates that the speaker is weighing up and valuing the other person's comments against their own opinion.

However, true listening incorporates a willingness to change – that is, allowing ourselves the potential to change our mind or understanding. Even if the other person seems initially to have wildly opposing viewpoints to ours, we can still learn something from them. At the very least we can learn to have a better understanding about why they might have such viewpoints.

We can learn a lot if we cultivate real curiosity about what someone else thinks and why, instead of closing our mind to their differing opinion. Although this may at first seem as though we are less sure of ourselves or our views, in fact the opposite is true, because a reluctance to listen carefully to others actually stems from an insecurity about ourselves. Perhaps we think that if we acknowledge differing viewpoints our own outlook will somehow be undermined. We secretly fear that our own view can't withstand the existence of other views – so we try to deny them and block them out, and in so doing we may secretly label the other person as 'stupid' or 'thickheaded'.

ACTIVE LISTENING

The concept of active listening is employed in a wide range of therapeutic situations, including talk therapies, and by doctors, dentists, tutors, coaches and many others. It can also be used more generally in our day-to-day conversations with our colleagues, friends, partners and children. It will help us to communicate more effectively and encourages connection.

The use of the word 'active' reflects the fact that listening is a dynamic activity – where the listener needs to meet the speaker halfway. The hallmarks of active listening are paying close attention to what the speaker is saying, and trying to understand the meaning in the words, tone and body language. The listener may acknowledge the words with gestures and facial expressions. It often involves paraphrasing or repeating the words back to the speaker, which serves both to demonstrate that the listener is really listening, and as a check to understanding. The listener may also ask relevant and exploratory questions, and consider the feeling behind the words. During these exchanges the speaker may clarify their original statement, emphasise some aspect or even change their mind altogether.

> 'Oh, right. How did you feel about that?'

> 'It sounds as though it wasn't what you expected.'

> 'That's interesting. How does it work?'

Clearly a key aspect of this type of listening is providing enough space for the speaker to articulate their ideas. At this time we need to refrain from voicing our own ideas – we need to keep silent. This silence is not, however, only about waiting for the speaker to finish so that we can say our own piece – it is a kind of silence of emptiness, where we let go of our own viewpoint for a moment and try to see the world through the speaker's eyes. Active listening is not a set of techniques or rules to apply to conversation: it needs to be based on a real acceptance and curiosity about the other person's experience. If it is not, it will come across as condescending and inauthentic.

Having said all this, listening actively does not necessarily mean that you have to agree with everything the speaker has to say. At times of conflict you almost certainly won't, but this doesn't mean that active listening is impossible or redundant. In fact, it may be the time when it is most important to try to listen carefully. If you allow yourself to see things from the speaker's point of view, it may be easier to express your own differing opinion in a way that will make it easier for them to accept. By trying hard to understand the speaker, you may find – to your surprise – that your own ideas aren't quite as fixed as you previously thought they were.

We have two ears and one mouth,
so we should listen more than we say.

ZENO OF CITIUM,
Greek philosopher, *c.* 336–265BC

LISTENING AS CONNECTION

We may hold the view that our connection with others is built on a basis of shared ideals and experiences – that to be truly 'in tune' with someone we have to 'think the same as them'. However, when we listen carefully we may find that this is not the case. If we let go of our own viewpoint (even if only briefly) while we respectfully consider another person's, we can find that even though the specifics of our opinions may be quite different, all of us are guided by similar motivations – to be happy, feel secure and feel loved.

Staying silent, letting go of our self or ego for a

moment and allowing ourselves to experience the world through another person's eyes can help us find a deeper connection. We can find that the shared experience of being human and having the same basic fears, longings and dreams transcends the details of what we think about specific issues. Once we are able to acknowledge a shared sense of purpose in each other, it is much easier to work together to resolve any outward differences.

Be silent and safe – silence never betrays
    you;
Be true to your word and your work and
    your friend;
Put least trust in him who is foremost to
    praise you,
Nor judge of a road till it draw to the end.

JOHN BOYLE O'REILLY,
Life of John Boyle O'Reilly, 1891

BEING HEARD

I have focused on the role of the listener, but what is it like to be on the other side – the one who is being heard, or not heard?

Being able to express ourselves is perhaps a fundamental right of being human. All over the world people campaign and sometimes even sacrifice their lives for the right to be heard. People protest against censorship that prohibits them from expressing their ideas in art and literature. Many have fought and died for the right to vote, and to be heard politically.

Why is being heard so important? On one level, we can see that not being allowed a voice may be part of a package of oppression and exploitation. Throughout history, those who have been denied a voice have also been denied other basic rights such as liberty and freedom from harm.

However, not being heard also affects us on a smaller scale, on an interpersonal level. Being ignored can be deeply upsetting. If it happens on a regular basis we may start to feel that we are unwanted. This can eat away at our self-esteem. We may compensate by acting out angrily or by attention seeking, or feel depressed and retreating into ourselves.

> The art of conversation is the art of hearing
> as well as of being heard.
>
> WILLIAM HAZLITT,
> 'On the Conversation of Authors', 1820

LISTENING AS CONTAINMENT

When someone listens to us they are not only acknowledging our opinion or our experience, but also acknowledging us on a more fundamental level. They are recognising us as a person. They are showing us that our opinions and views are acceptable, that we are acceptable.

This type of listening becomes a gift of unconditional acceptance. It does not mean that the listener necessarily agrees with everything we say, but that they understand and accept that we have come to think and feel in a particular way because of what has gone before. It is entirely reasonable for us to be the way that we are.

Unconditional acceptance is what mothers (and fathers) offer as they hold their newborn babies in their arms. They allow their babies to be however they are. In therapeutic terms this is known as containment. True listening is a way of containing the speaker. We are no longer babies but still benefit from being held in this way. None of us is perfectly secure or 100 per cent confident. Most of us have taken knocks on the way to adulthood, and we may have self-defeating habits that prevent us from achieving our full potential in some areas of our lives.

The process of being listened to builds on the work that our parents did when they held us as babies. When we are listened to it helps build our self-esteem, and we feel more confident and valued. This happens wherever we find a listening ear: it could be in a formal therapeutic relationship, or in the company of our friends, family or even the stranger we sit next to on a train. Of course, in talk therapy the regular and confidential nature of the listening becomes a powerful tool for recovery and change. On a smaller scale, however, the listening offered to us by people around us in our everyday lives can also have a great impact.

EVERYDAY CONVERSATION

It would not be possible or appropriate to employ these techniques for active listening during every single conversation that we have in our day-to-day lives:

'Please can you pass me the mustard?'

'You'd like some mustard. How does
the mustard make you feel?'

In fact, going over the top and attaching too much importance to trivial conversations would be counterproductive. Your conversation partner would think that you were missing the point or even taking the mickey.

I believe that making an effort to listen carefully to each other really can make a difference to the quality of our relationships – but we have to do this with authenticity. By practising careful speech and paying attention, we can start to kindle our own natural curiosity in other people. With this in place, it will be clear to us when it is important to listen closely to someone's remarks and when it is appropriate to take them at face value. It is not our job to be the world's therapist but we can take responsibility for not causing more harm in the world. With a willingness to listen where necessary, we can make the world a more friendly and compassionate place.

. . . .

VISUALISATION

Unconditional listening

For this exercise you need to find someone who is not speaking. It may be a person who is sleeping or absorbed in an activity, someone who is unable to speak, perhaps due to illness or age, someone you know or a stranger such as a person sitting in front of you on a bus. You may do any stage of the exercise for as long as you like.

Sit near the subject and notice your breath flowing in and out of your body. Bring to mind that this being was once a baby, lying helpless in their mother's arms. As you breathe in, accept that, just like you, they were once (or are still) a baby. As you breathe out, wish that baby well.

Breathe in and briefly consider what hardships and sorrows this being has suffered, or will suffer, from the beginning of their life to its end. Send them a breath of compassion.

Breathe in and bring to mind the joys they must have already experienced and will experience in the future, just as you experience joy at times. Breathe out with gladness.

Now, as you breathe in, feel your chest open with acceptance for all the experiences that might happen – whether welcome or not. Breathe out and send this acceptance to the subject.

. . . .

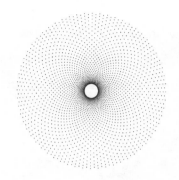

WHEN WE HAVE
NO WORDS

Speech is such a fundamental part of the way we communicate, yet there are many among us who do not speak. What is the world like for those of us who cannot talk, or choose not to? The way we relate to the speechless can tell us something about our own relationship with silence and the way we value words.

THE PRE-VERBAL CHILD

I have already mentioned the 'silence' of the womb (see page 77). Babies come into this world without the mental capacity or physical ability to speak words. By the time they get to their first birthday most know at least one or two words.

It is hard to say exactly what the world is like for the pre-verbal child. We none of us remember that time in our lives – or perhaps we do remember it but are no longer able to interpret memories from our pre-lingual age. As babies acquire new words, we can see that their relationship with a named object (or concept) changes. It becomes more distinct and fixed. Babies tend to point as they name people or objects – mama, dada, doggy, drink. It is as if they are defining both themselves and the world at the same time. As language grows so does the sense of self. That is a cup; it is not me. That is kitty; it is not me.

So in a world without words, perhaps the boundary line between self and other is rather more fluid. The act of labelling something is intrinsically bound up with becoming separate from it. We are then free to form a relationship with that thing. So during the first part of our lives we move from being an indistinct entity – nameless and 'at one with everything' – towards creating a separate self or ego as we build language. Interestingly, the spiritual path in Buddhism, and indeed in other religions, is to move beyond and transcend this sense of self. We might therefore think that it would be easier if we could just hold onto the pre-verbal state in the first place – but it seems that we can't just skip this ego-building step. We need to create a sense of self that is so strong and secure that eventually we can let it go. We will have trouble moving beyond it if it isn't fully formed.

HOW AGE AFFECTS SPEECH

As we move towards the end of our lives speech tends to slow down. Conditions such as memory loss can affect our speech – and it may be lost completely in severe dementia. And for those who are not suffering from cognitive impairment, there may simply be a sense that speech is not that necessary. Perhaps as we grow older we are not as quick to give our opinions as we were. According to the Socratic version of wisdom, we are wise when we allow that there are things we don't know. As we amass more experience, hopefully we also gain more equanimity – we don't get as worked up as we used to about things we cannot change.

We tend to think of talking as a fundamental part of being human, yet when we look at the span of our lives, we can see that speech is transitory, as we begin and end our lives in silence. For babies, learning speech is intrinsically bound up with a growing sense of self. Perhaps this process happens in reverse in old age – as speech becomes less important as a means of defining ourselves, the ego becomes less dominant. Recognising this link between putting forward our ideas and opinions and our sense of self and ego can help us let go of some of our attachment to speech.

Our culture has an uneasy relationship with wisdom and age. Although we might like to think in terms of the archetype of the wise elders, in fact younger people often act as if the opposite is true of older people. There is currently an entrenched belief that older people have inferior mental capacity. This is reflected in the pervasiveness of 'elderspeak', a kind of exaggerated baby talk aimed at older people regardless of their cognitive abilities. It can be heard throughout public places – in banks, at libraries and on buses. It is so prevalent in nursing homes that many people who live in them have become inured to it.

> 'And what are we going to have for
> breakfast today, Dearie?'

> 'We'll all have a jolly good sing-song,
> won't we?'

Some people find this manner of speaking comforting and nurturing, while others consider it disrespectful.

Some can find it so infuriating that they respond angrily – leading to them being labelled as 'difficult' and 'troublemakers'.

Becoming more aware of the way in which we speak to people can help us to communicate with more authenticity. At certain times it may be appropriate to speak in a familiar and affectionate way – at other times this kind of speech may be unwelcome and out of place. Moments of silence can help us to gauge the attitude of the person we are speaking to and help us to find the right tone.

Partly because of the stigma that surrounds the ageing process, many people fear getting older. This fear in turn contributes to a general lack of appreciation for the qualities of old age. A movement towards taciturnity is taken as a sign of being less productive and less able to contribute to society. It reflects our unease with this aspect of silence. Becoming aware of this prevailing attitude can help us to unpick our own assumptions about other people's silences. We can become more sensitive to the way in which we respond to taciturnity, and not just use it as an opportunity to fill it up with our own speech and opinions. We can take care to show respect for other people's silence and not mindlessly talk over it, as if it is a sign of vacancy.

LEARNING FROM ANIMALS

Many people seek out the companionship of animals precisely because they like their silent company. Animals are not only speechless; they also seem to be, for the most part, without egos. Humans have forged relationships with animals since the dawn of civilisation – there is evidence that hunter-gatherers domesticated wolves, the ancestors of all our domestic dogs, in Europe about 20,000–30,000 years ago.

It is perhaps not surprising that dogs and horses, both of which have served as our pets and workmates for millennia, are particularly empathic creatures. In recent years horses have increasingly been used in thera-peutic programmes. Equine therapy has been shown to be hugely effective even in cases of major trauma and distress, and with patients who find social interaction very difficult.

The interesting thing about equine therapy is that it works with horses that are allowed to behave as they would in 'the wild'. The horses are never ridden, saddled, harnessed with reins or fitted with blinkers. They are not 'broken in' and obedient. In fact – they are given as much freedom and autonomy as possible. Because of this they are allowed to respond to humans in any way they like. The consequence of this is that they provide completely authentic feedback. So if, for example, a client finds it difficult to relate to others because she has trouble picking up on social cues, a therapist can point out what is happening when she tries the same tactics with the horse. The client soon learns that if she wants to gain the trust of the horse, she needs to be very patient and pay close attention to how the horse is responding to her. If she is in any way threatening or disrespectful the horse will merely walk away. If she appears unconfident or wary the horse will keep back. Gradually, with the help of the horse's feedback, the client learns to modify her behaviour so that the horse learns to trust her and they can form a relationship.

Although the therapist certainly plays a role in interpreting and guiding the relationship, it is the horse itself that does the teaching – all without words. If we are prepared to 'listen', we can learn a lot from animals and the way they interact with us.

SPEAKING IN SIGNS

I have discussed how we begin and end our lives in silence; however some people never enter the world of oral speech. Deafness affects a significant number of us. There are many variations on hearing ability: from being hard of hearing through to being profoundly deaf. For some, deafness comes with age or through illness or accident. Others are born without hearing. Generally, hearing loss is viewed as an affliction. Yet deafness also presents an opportunity to develop a different way of interacting with the world.

Although it may seem to the hearing world that there is little to distinguish between acquired deafness and born deafness, in fact this difference has a major significance. For those that are born Deaf (with a capital D, as the Deaf community tends to designate it), English may not be their main language. Our first language is the one that we learn from birth. Deaf children cannot hear or acquire spoken language as readily as their hearing peers, so their natural language may be sign language. Because it will be learnt later, English (or the spoken language of their country) in effect becomes a second language. As a consequence, reading and writing is also more difficult for those born Deaf, because they have not acquired the language in the same way. It is more akin to learning, say, Latin than a spoken language. Deaf people may therefore not be fully fluent in the prevailing language, and the written word is less useful to them as a means of communication than one might suppose. Deaf children, on average, leave school with a low reading age and cannot access information through word of mouth or from the media in the same way as their hearing peers.

Sign language is a linguistic language that, in the main, uses manual communication to convey meaning. Sign language uses shapes and movements of the hands, arms and body, along with facial expressions. Body language is formed of non-linguistic communication and is quite different. Like oral languages, sign languages evolve in the communities that use them, so there is no universal sign language. Recent data has counted as many as 137 different sign languages. However, because of the way in which they have evolved, sign languages don't match the spoken languages of the larger community. There are even regional variations. So, for example, while Britain, America and Australia all have English as a common oral language, the sign languages of the three countries are quite different, with different vocabularies and grammatical structures.

- One in six of the UK population has some form of hearing loss.
- More than 900,000 people are severely or profoundly deaf.
- 90 per cent of deaf children are born to hearing parents.
- Around 50,000 of UK deaf people use British Sign Language as their main or preferred language.
- The first written record of a sign language is in Plato, 5th century BC.

Many thousands of people in the UK use sign language as their main language, and signing is a familiar sight on TV and at events. However, sign language has not always been accepted by society. In 1880 a conference in Milan 'On the Education of the Deaf' was attended by 164 delegates from seven countries (though only one of them was himself deaf). After six days of discussions the conference banned the teaching of sign language to Deaf children in schools worldwide. Instead, they were taught only to lipread and to speak orally, with the idea that this would result in them integrating more easily with the hearing community. However, lipreading is not foolproof – in the main it is only possible to catch about half of the words uttered. For much of a century, Deaf people battled through stigma and repression in order to assert the right to communicate with signs and establish their own distinct culture. Nowadays, educators recognise that Deaf children benefit from a more flexible approach to language, one that can incorporate a range of communication methods.

The ability to lipread and speak orally undoubtedly help integration with the hearing community, but the addition of sign language can offer a better command of language and ease of communication between those who learn it. British Sign Language was recognised as an official language in 2003.

It may seem amazing to us nowadays that for many years Deaf people were denied the right to communicate in a way that felt natural to them. Rather than accepting that a silent language following a different linguistic model could provide effective communication, the Deaf were shoehorned into an oral language that would never meet their needs in more than a limited way. Similarly to our attitude towards old age, I think this also reflects a discomfort with both silence and any departure from the accepted norm. Even if we don't suffer from deafness, we can learn from the Deaf community. When silence is imposed upon us, we can use this as an opportunity to develop alternative ways of 'being' with the world.

> 'Tis calm indeed! so calm, that it disturbs
> And vexes meditation with its strange
> And extreme silentness. Sea, hill, and wood,
> This populous village! Sea, and hill, and
> wood,
> With all the numberless goings-on of life,
> Inaudible as dreams!

SAMUEL TAYLOR COLERIDGE,
'Frost at Midnight', 1798

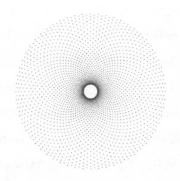

PUBLIC SILENCES AND
HOW WE RELATE TO THEM

In a world filled with noise, public moments of silence can be very powerful. Unexpected silences can sometimes be strange and uncomfortable. These silences creep into our everyday world and take on a deeper resonance. The way we relate to them can tell us something about ourselves.

DEAD AIR

I've already mentioned how we often reach for the radio button when we find ourselves in a quiet situation. In fact, in developed countries about 9 in 10 people listen to the radio each week. Many listen to the radio to 'keep them company' when they are alone, to relieve the boredom of driving or to add some interest while gardening or doing chores.

When the radio goes unexpectedly quiet the lack of noise can be unnerving and in some cases even ominous. These unplanned radio silences are known as 'dead air', and they cause much consternation among radio producers and listeners alike. Across the country listeners find themselves fiddling with the knobs on their radios in confusion, while behind-the-scenes broadcasters rush around trying to reinstate programming. When BBC Radio 4 unexpectedly went silent during an evening broadcast of Midweek in 2012, a tweeter wondered whether nuclear war had broken out.

Although the commentator was probably being

lighthearted, in fact this question has sinister conno-
tations. Trident missile submarine commanders, who
operate Britain's nuclear warheads, are thought to use
BBC Radio 4 as an indication of whether or not Britain
has come under nuclear attack. If they are unable to
tune into the *Today* programme for a particular number
of days in a row, they must assume that there is no one
left at the BBC able to broadcast and that British civilisation has been wiped out. In that case they must go
to the special safe on board the submarine and open the
'letter of last resort'. This contains the Prime Minister's
handwritten sealed instructions regarding Trident in
the event of a nuclear strike on Britain.

FREEZING UP ON STAGE

Unplanned silences in live performances can be even
more uncomfortable. A family member told me about
a concert that she had attended recently. At the beginning of the concert the audience sat in its seats waiting

for the music to start. Some shuffling went on, and perhaps some people cleared their throats. The conductor stood with his arms by his sides. The seconds passed. The silence became palpable. Was there some problem? A creak as an audience member sat back in their chair. What was he waiting for? Everyone's attention was focused on the conductor. A few more seconds . . . then he raised his arms and began the music.

This slightly prolonged silence had the effect of heightening the tension, so that everyone's ears were straining for that first chord. Perhaps this was the intention of the conductor, or he might just have been listening for the perfect silence in which to start the piece. When it came the audience's attention was in the sharpest focus. For a performance to truly excel, the quality of the playing needs to be matched by the quality of the listening – perhaps this silence was the conductor's way of managing the audience as well as the orchestra.

Unmanaged silences, however, can be acutely uncomfortable. This is especially the case when an actor dries up on stage. Actors report that the fear of forgetting their lines is the theme of many of their dreams. In fact, you don't have to be a professional actor to suffer from this dream. Many of us experience dreams about forgetting lines in a play (they are similar to dreams of, for example, sitting exams in the nude having done no revision).

'Corpsing' is a related problem. This is when an actor breaks out of character by laughing at an inappropriate moment. The term is thought to originate from the situation when an actor laughs while pretending to be dead on stage. Radio and TV broadcasters also sometimes face this problem at serious moments. They may be unable to speak as they try to contain their laughter, then burst out in uncontrollable giggling.

These types of unexpected silences can be acutely uncomfortable. Perhaps this is because they tap into some of our deepest fears. Radio silence can even suggest that the world as we know it is disintegrating. To a lesser extent, when we watch a play we agree to suspend our disbelief for the duration of the performance, so if an actor forgets their lines we are forced to quickly 're-surface' from the world that we have immersed ourselves in.

These kinds of experiences show us how powerful silence can be. When we are confronted with such silences we can take note of our own response and learn from that. In a brief moment, silence can cut through all of our assumptions about the way our world works and throw everything into doubt. Perhaps this is because in the back of our minds we know that silence has some kind of association with the bigger aspects of life. Silence heralds transcendence, the dissolution of the ego and, ultimately, death. Learning to accept those ideas is not a small task.

COLLECTIVE SILENCE

Honouring the dead with a minute or two of collective silence has become firmly established in Western culture. Perhaps the best-known occasion featuring this type of silence in the Commonwealth is the annual tradition of paying respect to those who have died in war on Remembrance Day – at 11 a.m. on 11 November. Across the UK and other countries, people observe the silence either in special services or while going about their everyday business.

On Remembrance Day the Royal British Legion starts the two-minute silence with the 'Last Post' – a piece of music played by bugle that originally marked the checking of the last night sentry, and therefore the end of the day. The two-minute silence is then concluded with another bugle piece, the 'Reveille'. This was used to awaken the soldiers at the start of the day. The period of silence in between is therefore symbolically a night vigil.

Across the world the moment of collective silence has become a standard method of honouring those who have died in other circumstances, particularly in tragic or shocking ways. The tradition is popular in populations that comprise peoples of different religious views. Because a moment of silence (as opposed to, say, prayer) does not ask participants to hold any particular beliefs, it is considered to be inclusive and accessible to everybody. In countries such as the United States, where state and religion are separate, and prayer is banned from state schools, a moment of silence is a way of introducing a space for quiet reflection.

Silences are sometimes held at a national or even international level, following a major disaster or tragic event. For example, on 16 November 2015, three days after 130 people were killed by terrorist bomb attacks in Paris, a two-minute silence was held across Europe. Respectful silences may also be held by specific groups on a local level, for example within an educational organisation or workforce.

Moments of silence are often observed at the start of football matches. Silence among tens of thousands of people can be an extremely powerful experience. The silence allows for private reflection and mourning, yet the shared group experience raises a kind of collective energy throughout the stadium. However, not all silences go exactly to plan – in fact they are very often disrupted by chanting, shouting and even booing. This can be in response to tension among the fans over the oncoming game. At times disruptive noise can be interpreted as a political gesture. When Turkish fans booed during a silence held for victims of the Paris terrorist attacks in 2015, their noise was interpreted by some as a response to the 'hypocrisy of the West', which had failed to similarly acknowledge the deaths of more than a hundred Turks at a bombing in Ankara just a few weeks previously.

In recent years a new practice has come into fashion in football, whereby instead of the traditional minute of silence, fans instead offer a minute of applause. Initially, when asked to honour the lives of notable footballers George Best and Alan Ball, fans spontaneously erupted into clapping. Since then some teams have specifically asked for applause rather than silence. Some feel that this is a positive alternative to the minute of silence as it allows supporters to celebrate the lives of the dead. Moreover, by drowning out disruptive calls and chants, it prevents the homage from being undermined.

Others argue that applause serves a different function from silence. Silence is special and at once both an individual act and a collective one. In a group silence, each single person has the power to keep or to break the silence, but when it comes to applause, if any single person neglects to join in the difference in volume will be negligible. Some critics suggest that the movement away from silence is an indication of a growing unease with it. Perhaps nowadays people find silence so uncomfortable that they are unable to keep their restraint and stay quiet.

Respectful silences in everyday circumstances can be even harder to navigate. If you are not in an actual service, it can be confusing to know when the silence begins and ends. Interaction between those who are practising it and those who are not can also lead to confusion. On Remembrance Day in 2014, an elderly lady was driving her car along Kensington High Street in London when she heard on the radio that 11 a.m. was approaching. She turned into a side street, pulled over in a safe spot and got out in order to observe the silence out of respect for her great uncle, who had died while protecting others in the First World War. According to her report, a traffic warden approached and told her she couldn't park there as she was on double yellow lines. When she didn't move he proceeded to issue her a penalty notice.

When I was 15 I worked as a barista in a coffee bar in a railway station. It so happened that my regular shift fell on the morning of Remembrance Sunday. As the station clock digits flicked over to 11:00, the station became noticeably quieter. Many people stopped in their tracks and bowed their heads. Not everyone, however. A woman in her thirties approached the counter and asked me for a hazelnut latte. I did not like to tell her I was observing the two minutes silence. Instead I took her order and her money with the barest of mono-syllables, and cringed while the milk frother screeched through the quiet of the station.

. . . .

VISUALISATION

The conductor

Imagine you are a conductor. As you enter the concert hall the orchestra stands and the audience begins to applaud. You walk through the orchestra, past the gleaming metal of the trombones and trumpets. The musicians are dressed in black, and their instruments are held upright. You pass the flautists and oboists and go on to the first violins, where a woman takes your proffered hand.

You ascend the podium. You turn towards the audience and acknowledge its welcome. Then you turn back towards the orchestra. You wait, listening for that perfect moment of silence. What does it sound like?

. . . .

THE CONVERSATIONAL LULL

Of course, pre-arranged silences are not the only types of silence that can occur in a group. Sometimes when several different conversations are happening at once, an unexplained quiet descends on the group and there is a moment or two of quiet before the talking starts up again. This can happen around a lunch table at work, in a cafe or in a classroom. There are several theories as to why it does so.

One superstitious explanation is that the lull occurs because all beings, whether consciously or not, pause to listen to angels singing. Another superstition from America is that these silences tend to fall at 20 past the hour, and mark the moment when Abraham Lincoln took his last breath (the president of the United States was shot on 14 April 1865 and died the following morning at 7.22 a.m.).

A more scientific theory could be that humans have evolved to pause in conversation every so often in order to listen out for predators or rival tribes. Perhaps the most likely explanation is the idea of the 'ripple effect'. As pauses are a natural part of conversations, sometimes adjacent conversations coincide with their pauses. When this happens, neighbouring speakers may notice the lack of noise and their attention is caught. They then instinctively start to listen to this unusual lack of sound, adding to the silence. The lull then spreads across the room in a wave, as more and more people listen to the silence. This is most likely to happen in an environment where the speakers are half expecting to listen out for something, such as a teacher in a classroom or the start of a performance.

SILENCE AS A NEGOTIATION

All of these ways of using silence show us how flexible and adaptable silence is. Silence is not just one thing. It is not a fixed concept that we can label as good or bad, or useful or not. In fact, silence has many different natures and guises: the kind of silence has huge implications on the way we experience and interpret it. When people come together they do a kind of negotiation (normally without any explicit acknowledgment) as to how they will use silence in their communication with each other. This negotiation is ongoing as we each make small adjustments to the way we are speaking. At times, silence becomes a kind of collective pact. In these cases it is very powerful indeed.

IN SUMMARY

In this section I have explored how we can use silence as a guiding principle in our interactions with each other in order to foster peaceful relationships. I have also considered how we relate to the silences of other people in both private and public.

The kinds of silences we experience are intimately connected to the way we communicate with other people. Silence can be used as an approach to speaking. It signifies listening, open-mindedness and, at times, giving way. By giving way I mean suspending our egos and opinions so that we can be receptive to other people's ideas and experiences. Such silences can be containing and nourishing spaces for both ourselves and others.

The second half of the section has looked at the different ways in which silence presents itself in our society. Since silence isn't our normal mode of being, when it appears it can be striking and at times even uncomfortable. I have reflected on why we sometimes feel uneasy at individual or group silences. Sometimes a lack of respect for the value of silence can lead to a temptation to push our own agenda when others fall silent; at other times silence makes us feel vulnerable and exposed.

Nurturing an inner silence

Out beyond ideas of wrongdoing

and rightdoing there is a field.

I'll meet you there.

When the soul lies down in that grass

the world is too full to talk about.

RUMI, PERSIAN POET,

13th century AD

So far we've looked at ways in which we can bring more silence into our lives through the places we spend time in and the activities we choose to do. We've explored how we employ silence as a tool in our communications with each other, and how silence might be interpreted when it is imposed on us in different circumstances.

Now we need to explore the idea of cultivating an inner silence – one that is not dependent on external conditions such as the environment we inhabit or the company we share. This is perhaps the most important 'art of silence'.

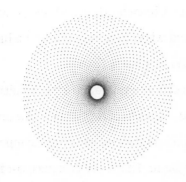

CLAIMING SILENCE
FOR OURSELVES

It is realistic and reasonable to acknowledge that our environment and our relationships will affect our state of mind. However, it is possible for us to learn how to be more peaceful internally, so that our happiness is not absolutely bound to these external conditions. We can do much to create the framework for a life that is conducive to peace and calm – but we can't do everything. Even the best-prepared among us will regularly face times when the unexpected happens and things don't go to plan.

We can't say no to every activity that crowds into our timetable, and we can't simply take all our belongings down to the charity shop. And, although we may be able to influence it, we certainly can't *control* the way in which other people talk to us. This means that we also have to learn how to navigate all that stuff so that it doesn't get the better of us. For that, we need to learn how to nurture our 'inner place of silence', which we can draw from even when the world is threatening to overwhelm us.

Creating a sense of inner balance and calm is not something we can do in an instant. We need to learn this skill over time, through regular practice. The idea that we can learn to be more calm may come as a surprise, as many people think that we are stuck with the personalities that we were doled out at birth or during early childhood. In fact, science has repeatedly shown that our abilities are not fixed and we can do much to improve the way in which we think, feel and act.

Working on our minds is not something that we have to consign to a particular time of day, however. It is not another chore to be ticked off (or put off until later). I have left this subject until quite late in the book, but in fact we can work on our minds alongside working on our communication, activities and environment.

There are three main approaches that can help us to achieve a sense of inner silence. We can:

· Learn to appreciate the silences that are already in our grasp.
· Cultivate a sense of inner calm and balance, regardless of the circumstances.
· Take steps to quiet the chattering of the mind.

All three of these approaches require us to develop a foundation of mindfulness. This is something that everyone experiences at times, though we may not use that word for it. It can arise naturally under certain circumstances – for example when we watch a beautiful sunset, or look out of the window in the morning to find the houses and street covered in snow. This kind of awareness doesn't have to be a pleasant experience that only happens once in a while. We can set an intention to *practise* mindfulness so that we are mindful more often. If we develop this skill we can learn how to use mindfulness to bring more silence into our lives.

USING MINDFULNESS TO HELP US APPRECIATE THE SILENCES WE ALREADY HAVE

I have already discussed how we often pass up opportunities for silence by reaching for our phone or putting on the radio. However, there are moments of calm everywhere we look, if we take time to notice them. If we learn to make more use of these silences, we may have less need to make changes to our environment or timetable.

The first thing we need to do is to notice. This may not sound like a very important task, yet *noticing* is one of the most powerful agents of change. Once we have begun to notice what is happening – in our actions, experience, thoughts and feelings – we can make careful, conscious decisions about the way we respond. We can use this in all areas of our lives. When we need replenishing we can notice the silences around us. We can choose to celebrate these pauses and quench our thirst at the well of silence.

If we don't take notice of the silences, or indeed of any other moments in our lives, we are running on auto-pilot, half asleep in our own lives. When we don't notice what we are doing we run the risk of reacting in a knee-jerk fashion to life, without giving thought to whether our reaction is the wisest and most helpful in the moment. If we drift through life without any awareness, we are not steering our own ship – we are not truly masters of our own minds.

This 'taking notice' is a moment of mindfulness – the quality of mind when we are aware of our

present-moment experience. Buddhism has many ana-
logies for mindfulness. It is described as the quality
with which a shepherd watches over his flock of sheep,
or with which a guard at the city gate observes all who
enter and leave the city. It is a quality of attention – but
not a fixed, concentrated focus that excludes all else,
which is something different. Mindfulness is more
expansive and receptive.

When we use mindfulness to take the time to notice
our surroundings, our feelings or the happenings of
the moment, we become more aware of what's going
on. These moments of awareness are what make us feel
more alive and more connected to the world around
us. If we are not aware of what's going on we cannot
appreciate it. This means that if we don't notice quiet
periods in our lives we can't benefit from the silences
they bring.

Mindfulness helps us to recognise our present-
moment experiences. If we don't pay attention,
beautiful, peaceful moments may breeze in and out of
our lives without us even noticing. Think back to the

description of the people crossing the marsh (see page 45). It was mindfulness that allowed me to recognise the striking, timeless beauty of the passers-by walking through the marsh. There is no point in searching for silence if we don't even recognise when we've got it.

Quieter periods may be long, but they can also be short. When we learn how to bring our awareness right into the present moment, we can start to notice and appreciate the gaps between words, thoughts and even breaths.

HOW TO RAISE MINDFULNESS

First of all, we need to make a commitment to mindfulness. That means that we've got to want more of it. We need to start recognising that it is helpful to us and decide to try to cultivate more of it. Luckily this is part of a virtuous circle. As we welcome more mindfulness into our lives we are better able to recognise it and more able to see how it benefits us. When we use it to help us find silence, we find that moments of quiet appear all around us. This in turn helps us to be more motivated to try to raise our level of mindfulness more often.

All of us experience mindfulness at times, whether or not we make any purposeful effort to do so. Therefore the first step in making an intention to practise mindfulness is to begin to recognise it and get familiar with the quality. The feeling is one of having presence of mind – of having your wits about you.

In contrast, when we are not being mindful we are oblivious to the present moment and what's going on. Instead of being aware that things have quietened down and silence has arisen, we are thinking about something else. Very often, we are absorbed in an internal fantasy – perhaps we worry about something in the future or go over events of the past. We may get caught up in thoughts and feelings, and not notice that this is happening. This can lead to us acting out in unwise ways – losing our cool, and making it harder to foster the spirit of silence.

When we set out to practise mindfulness, what we need to do is notice when our mind slips into forgetfulness. The wonderful thing is that as soon as we notice that our mind is caught up in something, this in itself is the return of mindfulness.

For now she need not think of anybody. She could be herself, by herself. And that was what now she often felt the need of – to think; well not even to think. To be silent; to be alone. All the being and the doing, expansive, glittering, vocal, evaporated; and one shrunk, with a sense of solemnity, to being oneself, a wedge-shaped core of darkness, something invisible to others ... and this self having shed its attachments was free for the strangest adventures.

VIRGINIA WOOLF,

To the Lighthouse, 1927

USING THE BREATH AS AN ANCHOR IN MINDFULNESS PRACTICE

Mindfulness can potentially exist at any time – whatever we are thinking or doing. However, when we are not specifically using our minds to figure out some problem in the past or future, then the present moment is the ideal resting place. When we come right into the present moment we may be surprised to find that it is more silent than we expect.

Sometimes the present moment is difficult to find – but we can use the breath as a guide to do so. The breath is a particularly good marker as it is always present and always unique. It is always happening in the here and now, so every time we bring our mind back to it we are anchoring our mind in a present-moment experience. The breath also makes us aware of our body, which we are apt to forget as we get caught up in our thoughts. Moreover, it emphatically links us to the outside world – this exchange of gases is fundamental to our life – and we are intrinsically connected to the world around us. It has been with us since the day we were born and will remain with us until we die. Although on one level the breath is extraordinarily simple, on another it is full of nuance and subtlety. That makes it an excellent object of our attention at every level.

We can make an intention to be aware of our breath all the time, at any time. Inevitably, though, we soon forget what we are doing and our thoughts wander off in another direction, often to the past or future, or some other imagined scenario. Bringing our attention back to our breath helps mindfulness to arise again, and mental distractions pass through us. When we set out to bring our attention to the present moment over and over again, we can describe this activity as 'practising mindfulness'. Soon, the process becomes a mental habit, and mindfulness arises more easily and more often. Our minds, now sensitive to the quality of each moment, will be all the more able to appreciate the silences that arise.

Despite our best intentions, however, it is often difficult to remember to be mindful and we may find ourselves becoming oblivious to the process for long periods. We can help things along by setting aside specific times to practise. One of the best ways to do this is by sitting quietly for a few minutes each day, simply with the intention of keeping the attention on the breath, for example. This type of sitting practice is what is meant by the term meditation. We can meditate at any time of the day, for as long or short a period as we want, in whatever the conditions happen to be. However, sitting in silence in formal meditation and establishing a formal time for silence each day, without other distractions, helps us to stay focused and committed to the practice.

If you make a habit of meditating regularly – perhaps a few minutes each day – this is a bit like exercising a muscle. We get more and more familiar with mindfulness – we know what it feels like and can spot it when we have it. This makes it much easier to raise at any other time of the day, no matter how noisy the environment and even if the circumstances are difficult.

. . . .

EXERCISE

A meditation practice

Set aside some time when you will not be disturbed. Find a quiet place. You can sit on a chair or a cushion on the floor. Ensure that your back is straight (but not rigid). It can help to tip your pelvis forwards by raising your bottom on a firm cushion. Sitting up straight can greatly aid mental attention, and the position serves as a reminder to you to stay on the task.

Close your eyes and take a few moments to run your mind through your body from the top of your head down to your feet. Lightly make a note of each area of your body, and allow the muscles to relax and settle into position.

Become aware of your breath. Gently allow it to lengthen until it fills your whole chest on the in breath and empties completely on the out breath. Follow the breath in and out of your body. Notice how your chest expands and contracts. With the same relaxed long breath, let your attention come to rest on the place where the air first touches your body – the skin of your nostrils or perhaps your upper lip. Notice how the air is cooler on the in breath and warmer on the out breath.

Lightly keep your attention on this place. Whenever you notice that your mind has wandered, gently but firmly bring your attention back to the breath on your nostrils. Continue like this for several minutes – ideally for a predetermined time.

Then allow your attention to follow your breath in and out of your chest again. Slowly let your breath return to its normal length. When you are ready, finish the practice.

. . . .

Once we have become familiar with the task of return-
ing our attention to the breath, this is something that
we can do at literally any time of the day. We may
not be able to find silent moments in every minute of
the day, but we will be able to find something of their
essence wherever we look. Silence is about cultivating
a spirit of receptivity, a watchfulness, an openness and
the ability to listen. We can't do these things without
mindfulness. Moreover, these qualities are useful no
matter how noisy the environment. In fact, you may
find that it is worth trying to conjure mindfulness *all*
the time – at least whenever you remember. Keeping a
light awareness of our breath doesn't interfere with us
going about our business, and in fact makes us much
more competent and efficient. When we bring mindfulness to each moment, we are truly present in our own
lives and masters of them.

SETTING THE RIGHT CONDITIONS FOR FACILITATING MINDFULNESS

On page 144, I talked about how we can work on our minds alongside making other adjustments to our lives – for instance in the activities we do and the way in which we relate to others. Some places and activities are more conducive to mindfulness than others. There is no shame in soliciting the most helpful kind of environment. You don't have to deliberately set yourself a challenge to practise mindfulness in the most challenging conditions. For example, natural surroundings are clearly very conducive to mindfulness and feeling peaceful. There are no egos in nature – the leaves do not complain when it is their turn to fall from the trees in the autumn, and the birds do not have an agenda as they sing their dawn chorus. However, if we were to claim that being in a natural environment is essential to mindfulness, that could lead us to make excuses (similarly to thinking that we can only access nature in far-flung destinations).

The fact is that mindfulness, which is what leads us to appreciate silence, can be practised *anywhere* and at *any time*. As discussed earlier, many spiritual journeys have been made inside barren caves – which while not unnatural, are not exactly abundant with flora and fauna. Formal meditation is very often done with our eyes closed. If we can't even see our surroundings they are clearly not a fundamental part of the process.

Why, then, do we bother to go for a walk or contemplate a flower in the garden when we could just as easily sit in a basement flat with the curtains drawn? The truth is that we don't have to set any specific preconditions for finding silence – natural or not. However, it is also true to say that we humans find some pathways easier than others. Most of us find that a pleasant walk puts us in a more peaceful frame of mind than does sitting cooped up indoors. Seeking out wholesome experiences is a way of acknowledging that. It's important, though, not to get hung up on the specifics, because if for some reason we can't enjoy life in quite the way we'd like – for example if our health or mobility restricts us, or we live in the 'wrong' part of town – we can become defeatist and may feel it is not worth trying.

EXPANDING MOMENTS

We can use mindfulness in this way to expand each and every moment. Mindfulness can help us to find the silence that is available to us right now. Rather than looking for silence as a set notion – whether that is to do with the level of noise or the length of time a silence lasts – we can try to look for *any* kind of silence. I like to think of mindfulness as a way of *penetrating the depths* of each moment – it's rather like holding the breath and plunging down into the water to search for a pearl. If we are not open to the possibility of finding the pearl, we can never discover it.

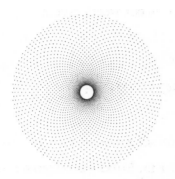

CULTIVATING A SENSE OF
INNER CALM AND BALANCE

So far this part of the book has focused on cultivating mindfulness as a means to get more out of each moment. It can help us to recognise and appreciate moments of silence, rather than continually spinning obliviously from one moment to the next.

Mindfulness can also help us to intercept judgements

and labelling, which in turn leads us to be more balanced and less likely to be ruffled by events beyond our control. This basis of calm involves retaining something of the essence of silence, regardless of the circumstances.

HOW WE CATEGORISE NOISE

Most people, whether consciously or unconsciously, divide noises into two categories: *good* noises and *bad* noises. 'Good' noises are the ones that we don't mind hearing – the ones that we might accept when we are looking for silence. 'Bad' noises are the opposite. They detract from the peace and quiet and set us on edge. The specifics of how we divide up noises into these two categories are of course unique to each person, because we each of us have different associations with different noises. As a general rule, however, people tend to think of natural noises as the good type and man-made noises as the bad type, though there are some exceptions.

Examples of good noises may include the sounds of wind in the trees, water trickling, birds chirping and sheep bleating. Bad noises might include the sounds of traffic, a fly buzzing at a window, a hovering helicopter, a car alarm, a pneumatic drill and the thudding base of someone's stereo.

If a noise is painfully loud or shrill it is quite easy to see why it might go on the bad list, but some of the noises that we consider undesirable are in fact not much different from the good noises. Take the noise of the sea, for example. Most people find this noise pretty pleasant. Depending on the distances and the wind levels involved, the sea can sound very similar to a motorway – but motorways are on most people's bad list, a bias that is clearly reflected in property prices.

If we bring mindfulness to our perception of hearing, we have a chance to intercept this process and notice a noise without leaping straight to the act of labelling and categorising it. If we start to react to the noise, we can notice that and just move back to the noise itself. That means that we can simply *hear* the noise. After all, noises are only vibrations. They are not good or bad.

This simple act of noticing and refraining from judgement can have a huge impact on the way we perceive noise. If we refrain from labelling noises as bad, we might find that silence comes to us much more easily because we are no longer distracted by negative feelings surrounding particular noises. When I was younger I sometimes used to have trouble sleeping at night. This was especially the case if I was staying in a strange place such as a hotel, or if my neighbours were partying into the small hours. When I learnt to stop judging noises the change seemed almost miraculous. I still heard the sound but it no longer bothered me. Once I could stop worrying about the noise I could stop focusing on it, so it no longer kept me awake.

Clinging to an ideal of a perfect silence inevitably results in disappointment and frustration as we can never hope to achieve it. Letting go of that ideal silence, and of categorising sounds into good or bad noises, can enable us to connect to a much deeper peacefulness.

. . . .

EXERCISE

Exploring noise

Go to a place where you can hear a range of different sounds but can sit undisturbed by others for a while. Listen for a few moments and try to detect where the noises are coming from. Choose a noise that you might ordinarily think of as pleasant. Focus on that noise. Hear the range and intensity. Hear how it comes and goes, if it does. Explore the noise. If it is helpful to you, bring to mind how you might make an abstract painting of the noise.

Now pick out another noise. Find one that you might ordinarily categorise as unpleasant or annoying. Spend some time exploring this noise without any judgement. How does it come and go? Does it interact with the other noises? What shapes and colours would you use to paint it? How does it change in pitch? Stay with the noise and allow it to be as it is.

. . . .

It's not just noise that we have a tendency to label as good or bad – in fact we categorise most of our experiences in this way. Learning how to bring a non-judgemental mindfulness to our experiences can help us to maintain a sense of inner calm throughout life's challenges.

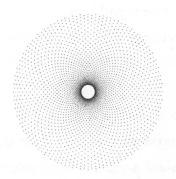

STILLING THE VOICE
IN OUR HEAD

Even in the quietest room and even in the dead of night, we are surrounded by sound. The interesting thing is that we don't hear much of it. When I did the exercise of noting the sounds within earshot (see page 165), it took me several minutes of listening before I could detect the most familiar and repetitive background sounds (such as my breathing, the wind rustling through the bushes and the faint buzzing of electrical appliances). This is quite a common phenomenon: our brains have evolved to listen out for special or unusual sounds – ones that might indicate danger – and to let other, more familiar sounds slip away from our attention. This helps us to concentrate on the task at hand. If we were to evaluate every single sound with equal weighting, we might find ourselves jumping out of our seats every time we heard a car go by.

It seems that we are selective with our hearing. As we get more and more engrossed in a particular matter, other thoughts settle down and diminish. We also acknowledge sounds and other stimuli less, until we don't hear them at all. Clearly, our eardrums are still vibrating in the same way, yet our brain no longer seems to interpret the vibrations as sound. This suggests an interesting idea: perhaps it is possible to 'tune out' all of the sounds around us and listen only to the silence.

It is easy in the world to live after the
world's opinion; it is easy in solitude to live
after our own; but the great man is he who
in the midst of the crowd keeps with perfect
sweetness the independence of solitude.

RALPH WALDO EMERSON,
'Self-Reliance', 1841

There is a hitch in this plan to turn down the volume
on external sounds: there's another noise that we have
to contend with. Perhaps the most incessant prattling
of all comes from the voice inside our head. Even after
we have managed to get away from our digital devices,
this inner voice keeps up a constant monologue, discussing the events of the moment, going over the past or
planning for the future. Sometimes the voice takes part
in imagined conversations. At other times it provides
a running commentary. The commentary can be kind,
but it can also be harsh or critical.

We have a tendency to identify very strongly with

this voice, especially when it sounds exactly like our spoken voice. For some of us it may even come as a surprise that we have an inner voice – until a few years ago I had no idea that I had one. I thought that the voice was just, well . . . *me*. I also thought that everything the voice said was correct (though I didn't really think about it but just let the voice call the shots). Because I was so used to it, it didn't strike me as odd that the voice could change its mind at the drop of a hat or react inconsistently to events.

Our relationship with this inner voice is extremely important in our quest for silence. The way we manage it, or are managed by it, affects our ability to live peacefully with ourselves and harmoniously with others.

With regular meditation practice we can start to tame this unruly inner voice. In the meditation example on page 155, we used the breath as the object of meditation. The mind always takes something as its object, and in this example we keep directing the mind back to the breath so that the breath can serve as an anchor for the mind. As we continue to do this, eventually the mind begins to settle down and thoughts come less often. Being able to hold our attention on the place where the breath touches the body requires concentration, and this is one of the main skills that we practise in the meditation. Instead of swishing off all over the place, the mind can learn to become more deeply interested in the subtle nuances of the breath. This state of calm concentration can feel surprisingly pleasant. We may amaze ourselves at how deeply we can immerse ourselves in this silence, and at how following the breath can be so enjoyable.

Distracting thoughts may still take you away from the breath at times, but eventually, with more practice, this may happen less often and your thoughts may be less hurried and agitated. Gaps between thoughts can lengthen. Sometimes there may be moments when you notice that the voice is silent. In states of very deep meditation, advanced meditators have reported that the body and mind are so completely still that even breathing may be suspended.

Developing mindfulness along with concentration and calm can help us to become discerning and pertinent in the way that we direct our minds. As suggested on page 165, with practice it may be possible for us to choose to focus at will on different sounds within a range – or even on no sound at all. This skill could have vast potential for the seeker of silence. If we could 'fade out' sounds as we choose, silence could be at our beck and call.

If, when we feel the first familiar itches of boredom, instead of reaching for our phone (or eating, shopping or scrolling through the Internet), we reach instead for the breath, we can start to penetrate each moment more fully. That way we may start to find a silence of our own – a silence that is always at hand. If we embrace those moments and sit with them quietly, we may start to make contact with something of our own true nature. It is only when we are able to let go of distractions that emptiness can arise – and it is in that emptiness that we may find a deeper meaning.

The greatest thing in the world is to know
how to belong to oneself.

MICHEL DE MONTAIGNE,

Essais, 1580–95

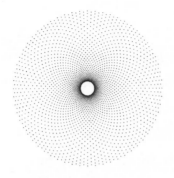

FINAL THOUGHTS

This book has explored what silence is, what it means to us and how we might go about finding it.

As an idea, silence is attractive: without even really thinking about what it means we know that we need silence. We have realised that we have become trapped in a never-ending cycle of communication, stimulation and consumption. Intuitively we know that *more* of the same won't fix matters. What we need is something radical: what we need is *less*. Perhaps what we really need is *nothing*.

However, searching for *nothing* requires a major shift in our usual modes of thinking and being. As much as we'd like to we can't just purchase it online or sign up for a course. Making space for *nothing* requires a dramatic alteration in our entire outlook.

We can start in small ways and the process of incorporating silence into our lives can be gradual. We've looked at how silence might be found in the types of activity we engage in, and have considered how we may be inadvertently crowding out silence with our jam-packed schedules, and thought about how we can adjust them. We've reflected on the peacefulness of nature and the solitude of certain spaces, and discussed how silence can be used in effective communication and how its presence can also be a source of unease.

Perhaps the central question of the book is: *how far do we really need to go to find peace and quiet?* The final part of the book explored the concepts of a sense of inner calm and silence, and included suggestions on how we might go about cultivating them through raising mindfulness and eventually settling the mind. Ultimately we have seen that silence is right here, within our grasp, should we choose to reach out for it. Silence is not a place that we must go to or a time that never comes around. It is an intention that we can make at any moment.

Because silence is so different from everything else, instilling more of it in our lives can bring about a profound change. Silence represents absence. It is so tantalising for us partly because of its apparent rejection of everything that our modern consumerist world stands for. Silence is about refraining. Abstaining. Saying no. Waiting, watching and listening. These are bold ideas in the modern world, which usually celebrates doing, choosing, convenience and immediacy.

Embracing silence involves stripping away the distractions and avoiding the stimulation. There is no longer anything to hide behind or immerse ourselves in. When we do this what we are left with is ourselves.

We are not always comfortable with that. Many people find silences intimidating and feel compelled to fill them – whether by themselves, with another person or in a full stadium.

There is something to be said for being curious about that uneasiness. It is as if we have a resistance to finding out who we really are. Perhaps we are scared of what we might find. Many of us are frightened of being bored – we imagine that we will find boredom intolerable, and without even thinking about it can find ourselves going to extremes to fill any small moment that threatens to leave us unoccupied.

Practising silence is a way of learning how to be more comfortable with ourselves. The more we know and understand about ourselves, the better able we are to work with ourselves and to lead productive, positive lives. If we are not always jumping to fill the gaps we can make decisions, act and even think in a more measured way.

Silence offers us an opportunity unlike any other: it provides us with the space to be in the moment, to connect with the world we live in and to allow the essence of our own nature to rise to the surface.

Now I will stop discussing silence. No matter how intelligent or thoughtful I might want words to be, they can never ultimately represent silence. Silence is something we have to experience for ourselves. Eventually we must let go of explanations and instructions and, like the pearl diver plunging into the water, put our trust in that wordlessness and dive into its depths . . .